Learning to Ride

By the same author
My Learn to Ride Book
Successful Riding and Jumping
Horses and Ponies
The Country Life Book of the Horse
The Horse and Pony Gift Book
Buying and Keeping a Horse or Pony
Caring for a Horse or Pony
Riding and Schooling
About Jumping
The Young Rider

Learning to Ride

Robert Owen

ARCO PUBLISHING, INC.

New York

Published by Arco Publishing, Inc.
219 Park Avenue South, New York, N.Y. 10003

Copyright © 1980 by Grisewood and Dempsey Ltd

Printed and bound by South China Printing
Co, Hong Kong

Library of Congress Cataloging in Publication Data

Owen, Robert, 1918–
  Learning to ride.

  Includes index.
  1. Horsemanship. I. Title
SF309.093   798.2'3   80-12781
ISBN 0-668-04976-6

Acknowledgements

The photographs in this book are used by courtesy of the following people and organizations:
Equestrian (Photographic) Services Ltd: Cover,6,8,9 right, 13,14,21,22,24,25 top, 27,28,29,30,31,32,35 top, 36,38,39,40,41, 42,43,45,47,52,53,55,56,58,63,65,66,67,68, 69,70,71,72,73,74,75,76,78,79,81,83,85,91, 92,93,94,95,97,98,99,100,103,104,back cover.
Sally-Anne Thompson: 6,9 left, 17,18 bottom left, top right, 20,24,35 bottom, 51.
Kit Houghton: 9 bottom, 11,59,106,107
E.D.Lacey: 15 top
British Travel Association: 15 bottom
Bruce Coleman: 18 top left.
Alfred Spencer: 43 centre, 85,87,94 bottom, 95.
Illustrations: Glen Stuart, Bill Bruce, Thelma Bissex.

Contents

1: Introduction to the horse or pony

Learning to Ride is a handbook of the horse or pony as well as a guide to riding. It explains in a simple way something of the anatomy, nature, and habits of the horse and gives advice on the essential routines of feeding, grooming and general care. It also supplements what is taught during riding lessons by explaining the basic techniques that lead to riding skill.

Most novices begin their riding career by having instruction at a riding school. That is the ideal way. Others learn to ride by enjoying the use of a horse or pony belonging to a friend. But, regular lessons and the help you get from friends cannot teach you all there is to know. People who have been riding for most of their lives readily admit they learn something new most days! The following pages offer assistance and useful tips, and aim to supplement periods of practical instruction.

Riding is fun; but it must never be selfish fun. The enjoyment must be shared by both horse and rider whether they are on a quiet hack or undergoing schooling. Horse and rider must act together if they are to understand each other.

Learning to ride
Once a rider can safely mount and dismount, and has acquired the ability to carry out transitions from one pace to another, he or she should work out a systematic programme of exercising to bring out the best in the horse or pony— and in the rider! The rider cannot hurry at this stage, but must show sympathy and patience. The horse or pony will be unable

Left: Returning quietly from exercise, these young riders are sensibly dressed, wearing jackets and hard riding hats for protection. The grey pony leading has an eggbut snaffle bit, and both ponies are being ridden in snaffle bridles.

to perform any exercise properly until he has become responsive to the aids (the rider's instructions), supple in body and calm in temperament.

A horse's brain is quite small in relation to his size. But he remembers what he is taught. When taught properly, he is a willing, cheerful and obedient partner. But he must be treated in a consistent way: he will show surprise and confusion if he is punished today for something that was accepted yesterday. And he must be given clear instructions. If the aid is not clear, why should a horse respond?

If you have knowledgeable 'horsey' parents or friends who can help you, and you have the necessary stabling and land, then owning and taking care of a horse or pony may not be a great problem. You may be able to afford to buy one before you learn to ride. Probably, you are not in this position. And if not, it is best for you to learn to ride under expert instruction before even considering ownership. Spend time – lots of time – with horses and ponies. Have lessons as frequently as possible. Learn as much as you can about feeding and stable management, and discover why grooming is more than making a pony look tidy. Feel in yourself that you have the patience and sympathy to ride well. And then, and not before, consider having a pony of your own. Riding well must be associated with knowledge, experience and common sense. And in that way it becomes something to be enjoyed by both rider and horse or pony.

Buying a horse or pony can be a most frustrating experience. But, done lightly, it can be more than frustrating to the horse or pony: it can be positively dangerous.

Far right: An ideal pony is one as successful as this. In Showing Classes it is frequently placed first in both the Leading Rein and Child's First Pony competitions. But such a fine pony may give no more pleasure to its owner than a much less distinguished one.

Right: Young people love to jump – and so do most horses and ponies. Here both horse and rider appear to be thoroughly enjoying themselves.

Below right: It is not easy to teach a horse or pony to come to hand. Sometimes a call and a handful of pony nuts will do the trick!

Below: A horse and rider enjoying their ride. Riding out forms an important part of daily exercise and is an important element in the fun to be had from riding.

Points of the horse

A new rider should learn the names given to the different parts of the horse's body as soon as possible. These are known as the 'points of the horse'. The importance of knowing them will quickly become obvious. During riding lessons, riding instructors will talk, for example, about a horse's shoulders, quarters or withers; pupils will, naturally, be expected to know where these are.

The points of the horse are also frequently mentioned in books about horses and riding. And they invariably come up in any 'horsey' conversation!

Another important reason for memorizing the points becomes apparent when a horse or pony is sick or lame, and the owner has to talk to a veterinary surgeon. The vet needs to know precisely where the owner thinks the trouble is. And his diagnosis and instructions for treatment may be intelligible only by reference to the points.

Below: The main points of the horse are shown here. It is wise to try to learn them all.

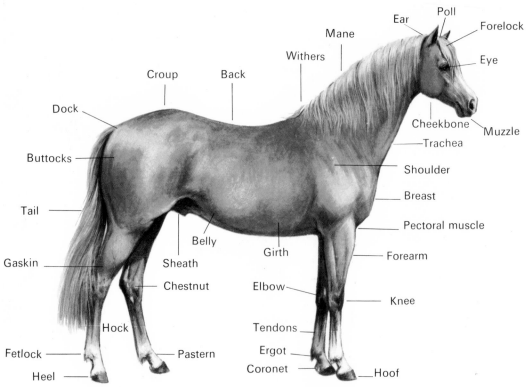

Conformation

In talking about the shape and build of a horse we use the word *conformation*. This word refers to the way a horse or pony has been 'put together'.

When we see a horse or pony for the first time, we gain an immediate impression of whether or not he 'looks right'. A horse with good conformation has the appearance of a perfectly balanced whole. But it is only after closer examination, and after studying individual features, that one can determine whether the first impression is correct and whether the animal is truly well put together.

Even very young riders – and sometimes people who have never ridden at all – feel that they can tell whether a horse looks 'good'. They may not know why they make this judgement, but they believe they can recognize the differences between horses or ponies with good or bad conformation.

It is rather like looking at a building or a book. We may not necessarily like its appearance at first sight, but we are able to sense whether there is good or bad design according to our taste and judgement.

Nature invites us to enjoy shape and colour at all times of the year. A tree can still be described as being beautiful to look at in winter, even though we can recall its beauty in summer. And the animal kingdom provides us with variety: the best having perfect or near-perfect conformation. But that does not mean that a horse with one or two minor defects will not perform honestly and well.

Below: Perfect, or near perfect, conformation is what every owner seeks.

Choosing a horse or pony

Learning to ride is but one aspect of horsemanship. It can be taught through lessons and books. Keeping a horse or pony, with all its complexities, is a matter for practical experience, and never to be taken lightly.

Those who are learning to ride may also be contemplating buying their first pony. It is vitally important to understand what this entails. Nobody should contemplate ownership until they have spent time working with other people's horses either at a riding stables or by helping a friend. The care and keeping of a horse or pony demands a good deal of knowledge. It also demands a great deal of time. Anyone thinking of buying their first horse or pony should read as much as they can about it, as well as seeking advice. Knowledgeable parents and friends are, in the early stages of ownership, most important. A horse or pony is a big investment; it is also a living creature for whom one is taking on responsibility. It needs some care and attention during *every day of every year*. If you cannot give it this, it is better not to take on the responsibility.

How to buy a horse or pony
When buying a pony look for one that is already the right size. Never buy a pony to 'grow into'. It is impossible to lay down rules about the correct height or breed. Young riders vary in height and weight. To suggest that a 12.2 hands pony will suit anyone between 7 and 9 years is rather like saying that they can all wear the same size of shoes!

Above: Horses and ponies can be bought or
sold in a number of different ways: from
dealers, at horse sales, from friends, or from
the advertisement pages of the specialist
equestrian journals. Reproduced here are
pages from the weekly, Horse and Hound, the
best-known and most widely-read of all
magazines devoted to the horse.

When buying through an advertisement a
telephone call should be sufficient to tell you
whether the horse or pony is the sort you are
looking for. During this first call make sure you
gather all the information you require before
deciding whether or not to go and have a
look at the animal. Ask about age and height;
ask about the breed and the pony's training
and experience. Never imagine an
advertisement will, or can, tell all! The
description of a horse or pony in such terms
as 'not a novice ride' will depend upon the
owner's interpretation of those words!

Left: A new pony, having just left the
trailer, is greeted by its new owners. This is a
scene which takes place many times each
week. It is quite possible the pony's previous
owners found their family had outgrown him,
and he is being passed on to a happy new
home.

Types and breeds

Long before horses were domesticated and later began to be bred for specific purposes, there were two main types of horse: the 'warmbloods' and the 'coldbloods'.

Warmblood horses developed in the warmer, drier climates of North Africa and Asia. They were light in weight, lively in temperament and much finer built than coldbloods. The heavier, more docile coldbloods developed in the more northern, colder and damper regions.

Once horses had been domesticated, they began to be selected and, in time, bred for specific purposes. Some were bred for warfare, others for hunting, racing and pleasure. It is this process of breeding that has produced today's many different breeds.

Grouping by type is therefore based on the size of a horse and the purpose for which it is used. For example, a hunter is a type; so is a polo pony, a hack or a riding horse.

A breed, on the other hand, is a group of horses or ponies that have been bred so that they will visibly resemble each other. Thus, an Arab, will always have a small, fine head, with widely spaced eyes, a tapered muzzle and well-shaped ears.

A breed of horse or pony has a breed society. All pure-bred horses or ponies of that breed can be registered in the Stud Register of the breed society. Some societies also register part-bred horses.

Side by side: a good sort of pony against a horse, giving some idea of the differences in height and weight. A pony, other than when competing in certain Showing Classes, will not exceed 14.2 hands. The smallest recognized pony in the world is the Falabella from Argentina in South America. This breed is so small it is measured in inches, not hands and inches, and stands less than 30 inches (75 cm).

Left: Horse racing is a popular sport throughout the world. Thoroughbred horses are bred to jump or to race in 'flat' races. A special type of horse is used in trotting races.

Left: Heavy horses, including the Shire, Clydesdale, Percheron and Suffolk Punch, are used for all manner of work. At one time millions were employed on farms, pulling ploughs and other farming equipment. Horses are still used today to pull carts through the streets of the larger cities. Cicero, the drum horse of the Life Guards, demonstrated the obedience required of these great animals.

Colour

Certain special terms are used to describe the colour of a horse, such as *bay*, *dun* and *piebald*.

In deciding a horse's colour, it may be necessary to look not only at his body but also his 'points' (when used in this way, meaning his muzzle, ears, mane and tail).

A horse or pony does not always remain the same colour. The colour of a foal or young horse may change as he grows older. Usually a settled colour will not appear for about two years; even then one can never be sure it will not alter as the years go by. The foal below, for instance, may eventually be the same bay colour as its mother.

Below: It is almost certain that the foal of this bay mare will change its colouring during the first two or three years of its life. Few foals remain for long with the markings and colourings they have at birth.

Horse Colours

These are the main basic colours of all horses and ponies. A more detailed description of an individual horse can be given by also noting its white head or leg markings.

Bay: Brownish body, often dark reddish-brown, with black mane and tail and black points.

Black: Black body with black mane and tail.

Brown: Dark brown body with brown points.

Chestnut: Reddish-brown body with mane and tail of similar colouring. Variations are *liver chestnut*, *light chestnut* and *dark chestnut*.

Dun: Body of a shade between cream and golden, usually with black points, and with a black line running along the back.

Grey: A coat of grey and black hairs. There are many variations. *Light grey* would best describe a white-looking horse or pony, like the one opposite.

Palomino: Body in any one of a range of golden colours, from cream through to an orange hue. The mane and tail should be silver or flaxen, like the horse opposite.

Piebald: Body with large irregular patches of black and white.

Skewbald: Body with large irregular patches of white or any colour other than black.

Spotted: Wide variety of base colours and spot colours.

Roan: Usually, a roan is a mixture of chestnut, bay or black with a light grey fleck throughout the coat. Three types are generally recognized – the *strawberry*, *bay* and *blue roans*.

Left: The term 'grey' describes all horses with a mix of white and black hairs in their coats. As the coat changes colour each year, the proportion of white hair increases against the black until an older horse can look quite white. But we never talk of a 'white' horse — these are always referred to as 'grey'.

Above: Palomino describes a horse or pony with a golden coat and a flaxen mane and tail. A Palomino Breed Society has been established and it will not be long before the Palomino is accepted as a breed and not just a colour.

Left: A black horse has a black coat, mane and tail. No other colour is acceptable except markings on the legs and head, as on this fine horse.

17

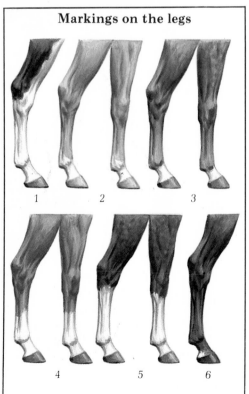

Markings on the legs

1   2   3

4   5   6

Markings on the head

Star

Snip

Far left, top: A Connemara pony with dun-coloured markings. Dun-coloured horses and ponies sometimes look quite yellow, and have black manes and tails. Most have a black dorsal stripe down the back.

Far left, bottom: A piebald horse has a coat showing irregular patches and shapes of black and white. A skewbald has large irregular shapes of brown and white.

Left: A chestnut is quite distinctive with a dark reddish-brown coat and a lighter mane and tail. There are three variations of chestnut: dark, liver and light.

Left, bottom: The markings found on the legs of horses and ponies. These are:
1 a full stocking
2 white fetlocks
3 white pasterns
4 white socks
5 white stockings
6 white heel

Markings

Some form of marking will be found on the majority of horses and ponies. Markings help to identify or describe a horse beyond a description of its colour. Certain terms are used to describe the markings seen on the face, head and legs. A horse or pony with no markings is called 'whole-coloured'.

The word 'patches' is used to denote an area of the body that has different and often irregular markings, usually of a contrasting colour to the overall colouring. For example, a piebald or skewbald is said to have patches. Mixtures of grey give a 'dappled' effect. 'Spotted' horses include the Appaloosa of North America, the Danish Knabstrup and the Austrian Pinzgauer.

White face

Stripe

Blaze

Wall eye

Measuring and telling age

Traditionally, horses and ponies in Britain have been measured in *hands*, each hand being 4 inches (10 cm). However, most countries in Europe give a horse's height in a metric measurement (though they have accepted measurements in hands). Before long, metric measurement will also be the rule in Britain.

To be measured, the horse is made to stand on level ground and a measuring stick is placed beside him. A reading is taken at the highest point of the withers. The measurement should indicate the animal's height without shoes; half an inch (1.25 cm) is subtracted if the animal is wearing normal shoes.

When it is necessary to know the height accurately, the measuring is usually carried out by a veterinary surgeon. In Britain it is possible to obtain a height certificate from the British Horse Society's Joint Measurement Scheme. An annual certificate is issued for horses and ponies of four or five years. But once a horse or pony reaches six years, it is possible for a life certificate to be issued, since at that age an animal is classed as 'fully grown'.

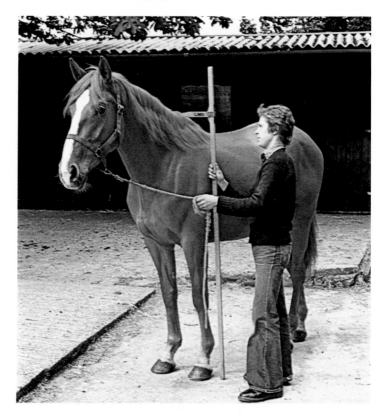

A measuring stick is used to determine height. The horse is made to stand on level ground and the bar of the measuring stick touches the highest point of the withers.

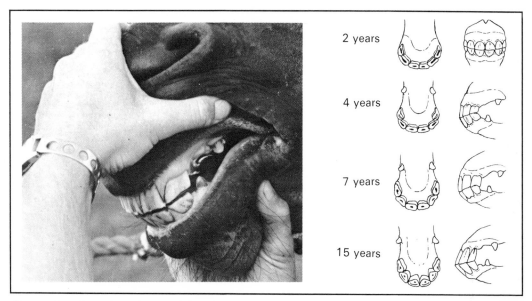

2 years

4 years

7 years

15 years

Above: Opening a horse's mouth is neither difficult nor dangerous, though it is not a good idea for younger people to attempt it without an older and experienced person being present. When opening the mouth use both hands, one for the upper jaw and one for the lower. Gently place the thumb and forefinger on the bars of the horse's lower and upper jaw, apply a little pressure to this point which lies between the incisor teeth and molars.

Hands and Centimetres

This table shows how to convert measurements from hands to centimetres, and vice versa.

Hands	Cm
10	101
10.1	104
10.2	107
10.3	109
11	112
11.1	114
11.2	117
11.3	119
12	122
12.1	124
12.2	127
12.3	130
13	132
13.1	135
13.2	137
13.3	138
14	142
14.1	145
14.2	147

The age of a horse or pony can be determined by the shape and number of its teeth. The first teeth to appear are the small, white milk teeth. These are seen within ten days of birth and remain up to the age of three years. From three years, the teeth begin to alter in number and form. The milk teeth are replaced by more, permanent teeth, these being somewhat yellow-coloured.

At five a horse will have what is called a 'full mouth', meaning that all its teeth will have come through. As the horse ages, the teeth alter in shape, and changes occur in the darkish rings that develop on their biting surfaces.

One noticeable feature is a groove known as *Galvayne's groove*. This appears between the age of eight and ten years and is found in the centre of the corner incisors. As the horse grows older, the groove develops, reaching down to the base of the tooth by the age of 20 years.

It is practically impossible for the inexperienced to be certain of the age of a horse after it reaches 12 years simply by looking at the teeth. A veterinary surgeon can make an estimate, but he will take into account many factors, including changes in the shape of the jaw.

2 : Looking after a horse or pony

Keeping and caring for a horse or pony is almost a full-time job. Horses need attention of one sort or another during part of every day of the year, with perhaps more time being given during the dark, cold winter months. Having facilities at home makes this easier and more satisfying. But, if you cannot afford to spend the time necessary for caring properly for a pony at home, it may still be possible to own a pony and have it looked after.

There are, in fact, three ways of keeping a horse or pony: at home, if you have sufficient land and stabling; at livery (that is, in a stable that will 'board' your horse in return for payment) where he is looked after, exercised and groomed and is ready when you want to ride; and at part livery, where the stable looking after your pony uses him for lessons or hacking during the time you are not riding, and consequently charges less.

Even a pony kept at grass, and many native breeds are quite happy to be kept out throughout the year, requires regular, daily attention. All horses and ponies enjoy company and appear to enjoy even more being regularly visited and talked to by their owners or riders. It is sensible to set up a routine and give your pony attention at the same time each day.

Right: Among the nine British native pony breeds is the New Forest. The forest is an area of southern England with many square miles of woodland, marshy bogs and open heathland. Although able to roam freely in the wide acres of the forest, New Forest ponies seldom move far from the roads and villages. They are excellent ponies—among the best all-round and versatile breeds in the world.

Horses and ponies at grass

Several matters have to be considered if a pony is to be kept at grass. First, the land: how much is available, what condition is it in, and what is the quality of grazing? Bad or soured ground can be treated, though this is a job for the expert and not one for the inexperienced.

It is generally said that a horse or pony requires at least 2 acres (0.8 hectares) of land. But that is the ideal! That amount of land is not always available, and frequently two or more ponies are seen grazing quite happily in smaller areas.

Water supply

A second consideration is: is there an adequate supply of water? Preferably, water should be piped into a water trough and controlled by a ball-cock. Using an old bath as a water trough is not really a good idea. Baths are difficult to clean and the water in a bath or similar container is seldom as fresh as it should be. During the winter months, continual inspections must be made to see that the water trough is not frozen over.

Apart from the need of good quality grazing (and in winter months a supplementary additive of hay) and a good water supply, any pony at grass will require some form of shelter. In the summer months, a field shelter enables the pony to escape from the flies, and in the winter months to have protection from wind and rain. The shelter must be properly sited, with the closed part set against the prevailing winds.

Fencing

Fencing is a problem, too. The best type of fencing is, without doubt, the post and rail variety, but many fields have good, solid hedges or stone walls that serve to keep ponies securely fenced in. Hedges, however, need a lot of attention, partly to see that no poisonous plants appear in them, and partly to check that no gaps are being opened by inquisitive ponies. It is a good rule to walk round the fences or hedges of all fields at least once a week to check for weaknesses, and to remove empty bottles or tins and any other dangerous rubbish.

A useful paddock with trees to give some shade. It has a sound post and rail fence which will keep any horses or ponies grazed here securely in.

Above: Two inquisitive horses, one with a
bandage protecting an injury, inside a well-
fenced paddock, watching a rider pass by.
Horses and ponies are always interested in
what goes on around them and are much
happier if they have companionship and a
varied life.

Below: A shelter, built with its back against
prevailing winds, is important for all horses
and ponies who are being grazed. It will give
protection against winds and rain in winter
months, and will be a refuge from flies in hot
weather. Unless the field has some natural
shelter, perhaps formed by trees, horses and
ponies will also use such a shelter to avoid
the heat of summer months. The shelter
should have a wide opening so that the
animals can go in and out easily and turn
around when once inside.

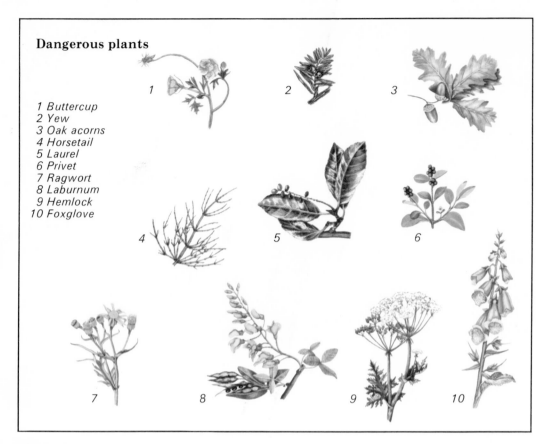

Dangerous plants

1 Buttercup
2 Yew
3 Oak acorns
4 Horsetail
5 Laurel
6 Privet
7 Ragwort
8 Laburnum
9 Hemlock
10 Foxglove

Above: Some of the plants that are dangerous to horses and ponies when eaten in excess. They must be removed regularly from any grazing field.

Right: In all paddocks it is best to have piped water to a trough. This is one way of ensuring that fresh water is available to the animals at all times.

Dangerous plants

Several common plants are dangerous to horses and ponies when eaten in excess. If they are seen in the ground or in hedges, they must be destroyed. Pulling out the part that is in sight will not solve the problem; the root must be dug out and put on a bonfire.

As with stable-kept horses or ponies, grass-kept animals must be looked at every day to see that they have no cuts, scratches or other injuries. The feet should be picked out daily. This will give an opportunity to look at the shoes and to spot any risen clenches.

It is not fair to any pony to leave him alone during the weekdays and then expect him to be ready and willing to be ridden at the weekends. A pony is not a machine, and an owner's or rider's true fun comes from caring for a pony who knows he is cared for.

Left: Barbed wire can be dangerous and is never recommended as a form of fencing for horses and ponies. Regular checks must be made of all hedges and fencing, and any broken sections immediately repaired.

Stable management

A stable-kept horse or pony is one that is kept in during bad weather or for most of each day and night. He is fed at set intervals and is not allowed to graze at will; but he may be turned out to graze freely for a few hours each day.

One of the practical advantages of having a horse or pony stable-kept is that he is ready for exercise or grooming without the rider having to go out in all kinds of weather in the hope of attracting him towards the gate and catching him! It may also be the best answer for someone who does not have sufficient land to keep a horse at grass.

Above: A stable-kept horse may be tied up with a ball and rope. This device gives the horse some freedom of movement and allows it to lie down.

Left: Horses and ponies drink a lot and a supply of fresh water must always be available for those that are stable-kept. It is not advisable to let a stable-kept horse drink immediately after feeding. It is far better if water is given before a feed. But this does not mean that a stabled horse should be kept without water during other times of the day and night.

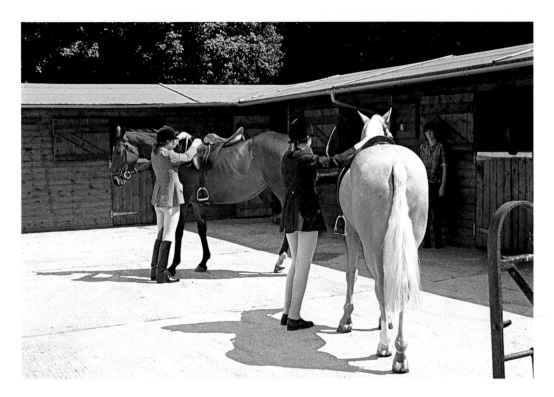

The stable

The box or stable should be large enough to enable the horse or pony to lie down without becoming cast. (That means, in this sense, unable to manoeuvre himself into a position from which he can rise.) And there must be plenty of head room. The stable must be light and airy, and care must be taken to avoid draughts. Although ponies stand up very well outside to all kinds of bad weather, they can quickly suffer from the slightest draught. Windows should be set high in the stable walls and out of reach of the most inquisitive pony.

The box must have a stable door, one that is made in two halves, so that the pony can look out when the bottom half is closed. Safety catches are important on the door. It is better to have two. One should be fixed near where the two halves of the door divide, and the other fitted low down and out of reach of the pony's head. It is surprising how many horses and ponies learn to open a catch by nudging it.

Above: Two well turned-out young riders have dismounted after returning to their stable yard. The roof of the wooden stables has a wide overhang to protect the stabled horses from the weather.

Stable facilities

In addition to the box in which the pony lives, other facilities are needed. There must be a *tack room* in which to keep bridles, saddles and all other equipment, and a *fodder room* for storing feedstuff. Hay should be kept in a *hay barn* set apart from the stable area. And, of course, there must be a muck heap, sited in such a way that it can easily be disposed of.

Cleanliness in the stable and stable yard is critical. A well-kept stable yard is swept thoroughly every morning and every afternoon. Good drainage is important in the yard, but drains should be avoided in the stable. They tend to become blocked, and are not easy to clear. If the stable floor is sloped slightly towards the door, life is easier when the box is given a thorough washing through, something that should be done every few months.

Bedding

Many materials are suitable as bedding for ponies, including straw, wood shavings, sawdust and peat. Rather than use dusty straw for bedding, it is wiser to lay down wood shavings. In fact, some horses and ponies fare less well on straw than on any other bedding.

Bedding, of whatever material, has to be attended to once or twice each day. Soiled or staled bedding should be removed by wheelbarrow to the muck heap, and all droppings should be taken away. The remaining bedding is then piled against the walls. The floor is swept, and allowed to dry until the evening, when the bedding is put down again to make a comfortable bed. Some additional bedding may be required, especially if a large amount of soiled or staled bedding has been taken away. Every two or three months, the condition of the bedding should be carefully scrutinized. If necessary, the whole lot should be replaced.

Stable routine

The routine adopted in order to carry out the various stable jobs will depend on the time available. The routine has to be constructed around the necessity for feeding and exercising the stable-kept pony properly each day on every day of the year.

First thing each morning, the horse or pony should be tied up, having been given a small net of hay to keep him occupied. Then he is examined carefully to make sure he has not injured himself during the night. If all is well, mucking out can begin, and the pony can be given his first feed of the day when the stable has been thoroughly cleaned. No stable-kept pony

Above: The floor of a stable must be cleaned every day. When the straw or bedding has been banked against the walls, the floor is swept with a hard broom and allowed to dry. Only when the floor is dry should the bedding be replaced.

should be taken out for exercise until he has had sufficient time to digest his feed. This will be at least an hour after the feed bowl has been removed.

On return from morning exercise, the horse or pony must be groomed. Regular grooming is essential to the health of the stabled pony. It is not a job to be hurried, and it must always be carried out with the well-being of the animal in mind.

A stable-kept horse or pony, just as one out at grass, must have water available at all times. The water should be fresh, and the pony should be given two buckets in his stable before his first feed.

Above left: A stable door should have plenty of headroom so that the horse or pony can watch what goes on outside. If the top of the lower door is edged with metal, the pony cannot chew the wood, an annoying habit known as 'crib biting'. The bottom door should lock securely with a bolt at the top and a 'kick catch' at the bottom that can be opened when necessary with the foot.

Above right: This grill-like extension to a lower stable door is known as an anti-weaving device. It is used to restrain horses or ponies from the bad habit of continually 'weaving' their heads from side to side. Weaving can also take the form of rocking forwards and backwards. It is a habit which is disturbing to other horses, who have been known to copy this nervous condition.

Feeding

Above: Feed should be stored in vermin-proof and damp-proof bins, preferably metal ones. When taken from the bins, the feed must be carefully measured to ensure the correct amount is given. After the horse or pony has taken his feed, the buckets or containers should be cleaned and dried and left ready for re-use.

Horses and ponies feed in the most natural way when they are grazing. But when grass lacks sufficient nourishment, supplementary feeding is required.

With the changing seasons, and every country in the world has its winter, there are times when grass contains nothing of value in the way of food. It is essential for owners and riders to have an understanding of the supplementary feeding needed in the late autumn and throughout the winter months. This is not to say that an understanding of a pony's feeding requirements is not also vital when the grazing is lush and plentiful.

The deciding factor when planning

supplementary feeding is the amount of work being asked of the horse or pony. Of course, his size and breed must be taken into consideration, but the way he lives is of primary importance.

The stomach of the pony is, in relation to the animal's size, quite small. It may appear that a pony at grass is continually nibbling at something, yet he will never go on eating until his stomach is really full. Ponies require to have a little in their stomachs at all times, rather than a lot at any one time.

Feeding supplements

An appreciation of what is meant by supplementary feeding goes far beyond a knowledge of good and bad grass, or good and bad hay. There are all sorts of feedstuffs to consider. Hay is an essential supplement to give bulk; but there are many brands of high-quality pony cubes and manufactured products that are fed as an addition to the roughage found in hay. Some are rich in protein, others in vitamins. Hay by itself will supplement poor grazing, but additional food is necessary to give a balanced and satisfying diet.

Grass-kept animals, during the late part of the year and throughout the winter months, require a daily ration of good-quality hay. Occasionally, for a special treat, they can be given a bran or linseed mash. And they must have a good, continuous supply of fresh water.

The stable-kept horse or pony poses other problems. His diet must be worked out with great care and consideration, depending on how strenuously he is being asked to work. Protein is important, and although pony nuts and cubes contain protein, not all are manufactured to a

Basic Feeding Chart

Feeding a horse or pony has always been regarded as an art rather than a science. Nevertheless, there are guidelines that can be followed. In work, it is recommended that a horse or pony receives $2\frac{1}{2}$ lb (1 kilogram) of food daily for every 100 lb (50 kilograms) that the horse or pony weighs.

Ideally the food should be divided between roughage (usually hay) and concentrates (oats, barley, nuts, maize etc with bran) in the ratio of 75% roughage to 25% concentrates; or in a 60% to 40% ratio.

This chart gives approximate weights of horses and ponies based on their height.

Size		Approximate average weight		Approximate daily amount of food when in work	
13 hh	132 cm	500 lb	227 kgs	12 lb	5 kgs
13.2 hh	137 cm	600 lb	272 kgs	15 lb	7 kgs
14 hh	142 cm	700 lb	318 kgs	17 lb	8 kgs
14.2 hh	147 cm	800 lb	363 kgs	20 lb	9 kgs
15 hh (T)*	152 cm	950 lb	431 kgs	24 lb	11 kgs
15 hh (H)	152 cm	1250 lb	567 kgs	27 lb	12 kgs
15.2 hh (T)	157 cm	1000 lb	454 kgs	26 lb	12 kgs
15.2 hh (H)	157 cm	1250 lb	567 kgs	31 lb	14 kgs
16 hh (T)	162 cm	1100 lb	499 kgs	27 lb	12 kgs
16 hh (H)	162 cm	1400 lb	636 kgs	35 lb	16 kgs

*T stands for Thoroughbred
 H stands for Hunter

This chart is produced with the permission of the British Horse Society.

similar formula. Some horses and ponies will refuse their feed if it contains one particular additive they do not enjoy.

Hay

Some owners prefer to feed hay to their horses and ponies by putting it on the stable floor. Others feel this is wasteful because the hay can become mixed up with bedding. But it is normally best to put hay on the ground for horses and ponies at grass, even though a certain amount of hay may be blown away or become wet and trodden down. The alternative is to use a haynet. This, when filled, must be tied to a ring high enough to ensure that when the net is emptied and hanging loosely, there is no risk of the animal catching a leg in it.

According to one calculation, a pony may eat up to 18lb (8kg) of hay every 24 hours. Assuming that this is the daily requirement throughout the autumn and winter months (say half the year), he will eat 18lb (8kg) × 7 each week. When the resulting figure is multiplied by 26 (the weeks in half the year), a total of 3,276lb (145kg) of hay is reached. And, on top of this, the pony will be eating some hay during the other half of the year!

Cereals and rootcrops

In addition to hay, many other natural ingredients can help to make up the diet of healthy horses and ponies. These include oats, barley, maize, bran and various rootcrops.

A pony should never be fed anything that is dusty or stale. All food, including hay, should have a sweet smell.

Oats

Oats are a most nutritious and balanced supplement. They are easily digested and most animals enjoy them. The husks must be short and firm and have a shiny look. Too many oats can make a horse or pony excessively lively, and care must be taken to see that the amount given is suited to the work being undertaken. It is not right to give oats to a stable-kept pony unless he is being worked reasonably hard.

Barley and maize

Barley and maize are a useful and safe supplement for horses and ponies. As with oats, they should be fed in small quantities and mixed with the usual feed.

Bran

Bran is perhaps the most common of all traditional foods used for ponies. It is made from the ground husks of grain. Bran can form the basis of a feed containing oats or barley, and can by itself be a most satisfying and enjoyable feed for all ponies. A bran mash is easily made. The addition of treacle or molasses makes it even more appetizing.

Linseed

Linseed, with its high oil content, is generally fed to ponies during the winter months. It improves a pony's condition and adds a lot to overall appearance. A linseed mash is beneficial for any animal which is not in good condition. To make it about a pound of linseed is boiled for three to four hours. By then, the grains of the linseed have become soft. About a pound of bran is added, and the mixture stirred to make a thick paste. But it is essential to remember that linseed *must* be boiled before being used as any part of a feed. And not too much should be given.

Other feedstuffs

Certain other items may not come under the heading of 'feed', but they are useful extras and when not given to excess, can do a pony no harm. Included among them would be root crops such as carrots, swedes and turnips, as well as apples and dried sugar beet.

Rules for good feeding

Many people with experience of horses

and ponies can give advice about the use of additives and supplementary feeding. But, often, younger and novice riders will have to rely on trial and error. An inexperienced owner or rider can always talk to a vet. He, knowing the local conditions and the type of pony concerned, will be able to offer the soundest advice of all.

The rules to be followed for good feeding include:
1 Feed little and often.
2 Keep plenty of fresh water available at all times, and give the horse or pony water before he begins to feed.
3 Keep to a timetable, and feed at the same time each day.
4 Feed hay each day, and see that the right amount is given.
5 Never ask a pony to undertake any work for at least one hour after he has finished his feed.
6 Wherever possible, give the best-quality feed available.
7 If a diet is to be altered, the change should come gradually. Never introduce a sudden change in supplementary feeding.
8 Allow a pony some time to graze each day.
9 Adjust all feeding to the amount of work being done. Never over-feed – always remember rule 1.

Top right: Hay is best when stored in open-sided barns, preferably sited not too far from the stable block.

Right: Haynets can be bought in various sizes. Good hay is light brown, sometimes with a greenish tinge. It should not be the bright yellow colour that most people associate with hay. Hay must always be crisp and sweet and should smell fresh and fragrant when a handful is held to the nose.

35

Grooming

Grooming, providing it is done correctly and thoroughly each time, will do more than give a horse or pony a good appearance. Its main function is to clean and stimulate, since the animal's skin is a vital organ, as important to health as a sound heart and strong lungs.

Of course, even hasty grooming will improve the look of a horse; but this is not the chief purpose of the operation. Regular and thorough daily grooming helps to prevent disease, promote health, maintain condition and ensure cleanliness, as well as improve appearance. These five aims must be remembered each time the grooming kit is taken out.

Animals living in a natural environment achieve something similar to groom-

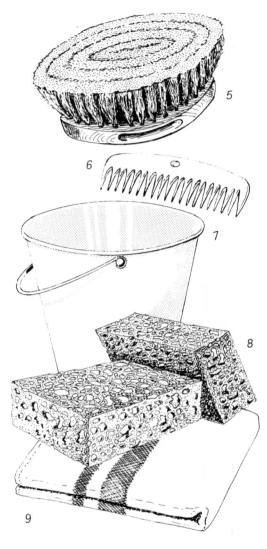

Below: Before beginning to groom the head of a horse or pony, it is best if the headcollar is removed and loosely fastened around the horse's neck. This will enable the groom to have both hands free, one to hold the brush, the other to guide his head.

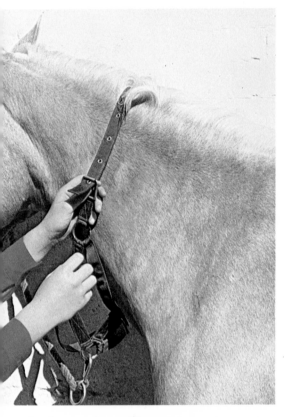

ing by regular rolling and exercise, and by rubbing their coats against trees or hedges. But, often, a pony that lives out through the year, or a stable-kept pony that is allowed to graze during part of the day, is rugged up, thus preventing a natural cleaning and stimulation of his skin. This, alone, is a very good reason for daily grooming. But a full grooming is really only applicable to the stable-kept horse or pony. The animal who lives out, especially during the winter months, requires a somewhat different approach.

The first requirement for a grass-kept

Left and above: The items that form part of a grooming kit are:
1 a hoof pick, for cleaning out the feet
2 a dandy brush, for removing mud and dirt
3 a body brush to remove scurf and dust
4 a curry comb, for cleaning the body brush
5 a water brush, for the mane, tail and feet
6 a mane comb
7 a bucket for water
8 two sponges, one for the eyes, nostrils and muzzle; the other for the dock
9 a stable rubber or duster, to remove any final dust

pony is that he should have a daily brushing to remove any caked mud. This also gives an opportunity to see whether there are any cuts that require attention. Then, the feet must be picked out, the shoes checked for wear and the clenches felt to ensure they have not risen. The thicker coat, which appears as the winter months approach, must never be too heavily groomed, for the dandruff and greases in it are nature's way of helping to keep the body warm and the hair waterproof.

Care of the grooming kit

The grooming kit should be kept in a box or plastic container. All brushes and sponges should be cleaned before being put away, and items of the kit should not be left lying in different parts of the stable yard or field. If kit is strewn around, it is certain that some items will be missing when needed.

Grooming routine

Grooming should follow a pattern; the person carrying it out must learn to enjoy the hard work as much as the pony will enjoy being groomed.

As a job, grooming cannot be hurried and there are no short cuts. The routine of grooming is logical and straightforward:

1 Tie up the pony and remove any rugs or bandages. Collect the grooming kit and two buckets of clean water.

2 Begin by picking out the feet, cleaning the area between the shoe and the frog. Work from heel to toe, and take this opportunity to check the shoes for wear and tear and for signs of risen clenches. Use a skip or wide basket or sack to take the dirt removed from the feet. This means that you will not have to sweep up before you move on to using the brushes and sponges.

3 Take the dandy brush and begin at the poll on the near side. The dandy brush, with its stiff bristles, can be used in either hand to remove mud, dirt and sweat marks. The action required is a

Left: The grooming sequence begins with picking out the feet. A hoof pick is used working downwards from the heel to the toe. It should thoroughly clean each foot, removing dirt or stones. During picking out the feet, it is a wise move to check that the shoes have not become loose and that there are no risen clenches.

Right: The dandy brush being used correctly. With its stiff bristles, this is the brush for removing dirt, caked mud and sweat marks. When using such a severe brush great care must be taken not to hurt the head and other delicate parts of a horse's body.

Below: Using a body brush. The curry comb is being held in the right hand. A curry comb should never be used in place of a brush.

Below right: Have one hand free of the curry comb when using the body brush on the horse's head.

to-and-fro movement. Take care not to use the brush on the more delicate parts of the pony's head or body.

4 Next, the body brush is employed. It enables you to groom through the hairs and down the skin. The body brush is not easy to use; plenty of effort is required.

Begin at the mane and, having brushed this to the wrong (near) side, brush the crest. Bring the mane back to its normal position and brush it through, seeing that there are no tangles or knots. It is suggested that the body brush be first used on the near side before moving to the off side.

Most grooms begin by taking the body brush in the left hand and the curry comb in the right hand, then change hands every few minutes. The curry comb is used solely to clean the body brush; the brush is drawn across the teeth of the comb.

Stand some distance away from the pony's body so as to be able to apply pressure. Use the brush in a series of short, circular strokes in the direction of the lay of the hair.

When the pony's body has been completed, turn your attention to the legs.

Then do the head: the headcollar or halter should preferably be removed and fastened loosely around the pony's neck. Some people try to groom with the headcollar in position, but this is never satisfactory.

In grooming the head, you will need only the body brush; the other hand will be required to hold the head and guide it to the position required. When finished, replace the headcollar, clean the brush against the curry comb and brush out the tail.

If you are right-handed, hold the tail in the left hand and release a few locks of hair at a time. These are brushed downwards until the entire tail has been groomed and is free from knots and tangles.

5 The body brush, dandy brush and curry comb can now be returned to the container ready for cleaning before they are finally put away for the day. If you now stand back to admire what you have done, you may think all is perfect! But there is plenty to do yet.

A wisp is now used as a massage pad to tone up the pony's muscles and put a shine on his coat. Younger riders may find this a difficult job because the dampened wisp has to be brought down on the pony's body really hard if it is to do any good. It is always used in the direction that the hair lies. The head, loins and legs should not be wisped.

6 Two sponges and two buckets of water are now needed. Preferably, the sponges should be of different colours so that it

Below: The body brush is cleaned by drawing its bristles across the teeth of the curry comb.

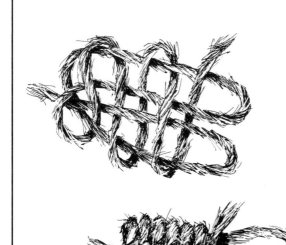

Making a Wisp

A wisp, when used energetically, helps to tone up a pony's muscles and put a shine on his coat. Preferably, it should be made of hay, but straw will do. First, dampened hay is twisted into a rope about 2 metres (6 ft) long.

Two loops are made at one end, and laid side by side. The rest of the rope is then woven in and out of the loops, each new turn of rope being pressed back firmly against the preceding turn. Finally, the ends are tucked in neatly. A simpler wisp can be made from a short piece of hay rope merely by forming a big, loose knot.

Below: To clean a curry comb, and to remove all collected dust and dandruff, gently tap it on the floor.

Below: To groom a tail, hold it in one hand and release a few strands at a time. Brush down through the strands, removing tangles.

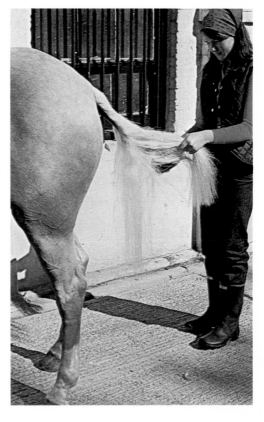

is always clear which is which. Wring out one of the sponges and carefully clean the eyes, muzzle and nostrils. You may, again, want to remove the head-collar or halter while doing this. When the eyes, muzzle and nostrils have been thoroughly sponged, use the second sponge to clean the dock area.

7 The mane is 'laid' by dipping the ends of the bristles of the water brush into a bucket of water and brushing the mane from the roots downwards.

8 The stable rubber, which should be folded flat into a pad, and may be dampened, is used to remove the last traces of dust from the horse's or pony's coat and produce the final sheen.

9 Hoof oil should now be applied to each foot, being brushed on carefully with a small paint brush. It will improve the overall appearance of the pony when it has been groomed. Hoof oil will also be of benefit to brittle or damaged feet.

Grooming is not a job that can be rushed. Experienced grooms take up to three-quarters of an hour each day to groom each horse they are looking after. This is a long time, but you should always be thorough, patient and sympathetic. If you are, then you will find that horses and ponies love being groomed. You, too, will learn to enjoy it and, perhaps as important, to be seen to be enjoying it.

When the sponge is being used to clean the eyes (above) or the nostrils and muzzle (below), be certain that it has first been squeezed out to remove surplus water.

Below: A separate sponge, not the one used for cleaning the eyes, nostrils and muzzle, should be used for cleaning the dock area. The tail should be lifted well up with one hand while the dock and the entire area around it are cleaned.

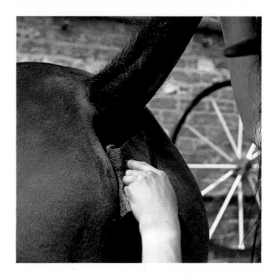

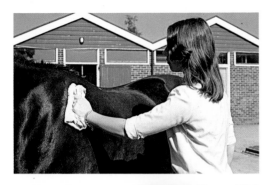

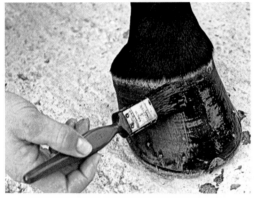

Left: A stable rubber gives a final polish and removes any final traces of dirt.

Left: Hoof oil is applied not solely to improve appearance, but also to prevent brittle feet. Brush on hoof oil when the feet are quite dry.

Below: Manes are pulled to thin them out or to help them lie flat. This is not a job to be attempted by the inexperienced, though many young riders can pull a mane once they have been shown the correct way. It is a job demanding patience, and should be worked to a routine—starting at the withers and working towards the poll.

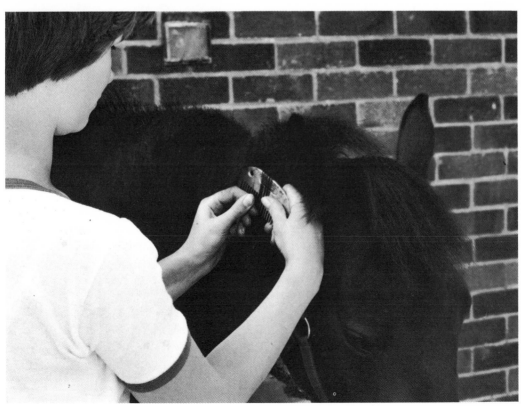

Clipping

Horses and ponies not kept at grass during the winter months will need to be clipped out. The first clip is given in the late autumn, and further clipping is carried out as and when the hairs grow again. If the hair is not clipped, the pony will sweat up and lose condition. Clipping improves the appearance of an animal; and, at the same time, it makes it far easier for him to be kept clean and well groomed. The three most common clips are the trace clip, the blanket clip and the hunter clip.

Using electric clippers
Before discussing clipping in detail, mention must be made of the need for safety precautions when using electrically operated clippers. Rubber boots should always be worn; never canvas or leather-soled boots or shoes. Neither the pony nor the person doing the clipping should be standing on a damp or wet surface.

Before blades are changed, the plug must be removed. It is not sufficiently safe just to switch off the power supply.

These precautions are not, of course, necessary with clippers worked by hand. Manual clippers are safer; but they make the work harder and slower.

Clippers, of whatever type, require regular oiling, cleaning and servicing. When not in use they should be kept in a box in a dry place.

Clipping patterns
Only with a *full clip* is a horse completely clipped out; but this is not often done.

Young people sometimes feel a little afraid to clip out. But it is not as difficult

Above: Clipping is carried out on all stable-kept horses and ponies, especially those who are in work. It prevents them losing condition by sweating-up and makes them far easier to groom and keep clean. Here, from top to bottom, a full clip, a hunter clip, a blanket clip and a trace clip. Clipping is not difficult, but younger people should not be encouraged to clip until they have been taught the correct way. Remember, never clip a mane, tail, or hair inside the ears, or around the muzzle.

as it appears, provided that it is done carefully. It is probably a good idea for a novice to be accompanied by someone who has experience in clipping – if only to make sure that the outlines are right!

The trace clip is the one used for a horse or pony that is turned out with a New Zealand rug. The hair is removed from the front of the neck and down through the entire underside of the body. The legs and back are not clipped.

The blanket clip is similar to the trace clip, but the hair is also removed from the neck and head, leaving the hair line where the stable blanket fits.

The hunter clip removes all the hair from the body other than a patch where the saddle is positioned. The legs are not touched.

Hints on clipping

1 Tie up the horse or pony with a halter attached to a loop of string, using a quick release knot.

2 Make sure the animal has been well groomed and is dry.

3 Check that neither the pony nor you are standing on wet ground.

4 Have a rug over the pony to keep him warm.

5 It is a good idea to see the pony has a haynet to keep him occupied.

6 Take extra care when clipping near the more sensitive parts of the animal. And, be extra careful when operating near the mane and tail.

7 Immediately the clipping is completed, put the horse or pony away and clean up.

Left The feathers of a heel being trimmed with electrically operated clippers. This tidying up of the heels gives a neat finish to the overall appearance of a horse or pony.

Rugs

Most horses and ponies are put at risk if they are not given some form of protective clothing not only in winter but also in summer. The native breeds are exceptions to this rule. They live quite contentedly at grass throughout the year, and seldom suffer any harm from extreme changes of weather or temperature.

Rugs, blankets and sheets, like the grooming kit, must be cared for, and never put away unless they are clean. If rugs are stored in a dirty condition, they quickly rot; and rugs are expensive to buy.

Night rugs
It is essential for the stable-kept horse or pony to have a night rug and, separately, a woollen blanket. Night rugs are made from jute or canvas, and are lined with a blanket-type material. The night rug gives adequate warmth on its own, but most owners and riders prefer to use it with a blanket for additional warmth. Blankets can be bought in many colours and are made from a number of different materials. For warmth and comfort there is nothing better than a blanket made from wool.

The New Zealand rug
A grass-kept horse or pony, depending on his breed and the facilities available, can winter out quite well. Provided that ponies are not clipped out and have a good shelter and plenty of room for natural exercise, it is surprising how well they fare during the bad months of the year. Their winter coat affords some protection, though during the severest weather there is need for a waterproof, warming rug in the night hours.

The most popular and efficient of all rugs for such purposes is the New Zealand rug. The better-quality rugs are made from extra-strong waterproofed canvas which, like the night rug, has a type of blanket lining. The rug is fastened with straps that go around the legs and clip back onto the rug, the front being secured by one or two buckles.

A horse wearing a New Zealand rug inevitably gives it a hard time by rubbing against trees, hedges or fencing. For this reason, it is not a good investment to buy the cheaper rugs; in the end the better quality will last far longer and is less likely to be torn.

All rugs, other than the anti-sweat sheet, are held in position by using a surcingle in addition to any fitted breast strap. Some, especially those used for travelling, require a roller.

With all its good qualities, a New Zealand rug should not be put on a horse or pony that has been brought in from heavy rain. The animal should first be dried with straw or towelling. Failure to do so can result in a chill developing, since the pony will have no chance of drying out once the rug has been fitted.

Day rugs
Day rugs can be bought in a variety of colours. They are frequently seen carrying the name of the owner or the initial of the rider. The shape of a day rug is somewhat similar to that of a night rug, though the day rug is made from wool.

The Lavenham rug
This quilted form of rug is light in weight,

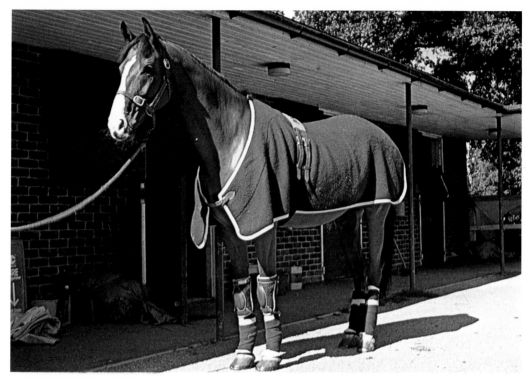

Above: A horse, well prepared for travelling, with a day rug and travelling bandages. Knee guards give further protection before the horse is put into a horse box or trailer.

yet surprisingly warm. A Lavenham is an elegant addition to the different rugs a horse needs. It can be used during the spring, summer and early autumn months.

Anti-sweat sheet

Made from cotton mesh, the anti-sweat sheet acts in the same way as a string vest, and prevents a pony from becoming suddenly chilled after return from exercise or work.

Summer sheet

Used, as the name suggests, during the summer months, it keeps away dust and flies. Although summer sheets are available in man-made fibres, the best and most practicable are those which are made from cotton or linen.

Above: Rugs and blankets are an essential part of stable equipment. This horse has a New Zealand rug, one of the most common types. A New Zealand rug is made with lined water-proofed canvas, giving excellent protection for horses and ponies who are kept out during cold or wintry weather.

Right: When a horse is travelling it needs a number of items of equipment in addition to the normal equipment at home.

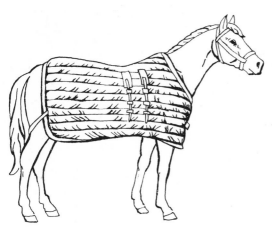

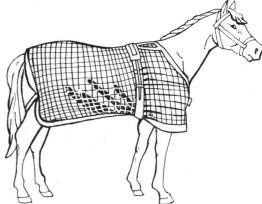

The quilted Lavenham rug *has been designed to give maximum warmth, yet it is very light in weight. This rug can be used at most times during the year. This one has a surcingle fitted into it to hold the rug in place. Nylon rugs are the easiest to keep clean.*

A summer sheet, *sometimes called a 'fly sheet', is usually made from linen or cotton. It is used for keeping away flies during summer months, and to keep the horse or pony clean. This one is held in position with a roller.*

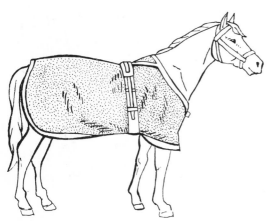

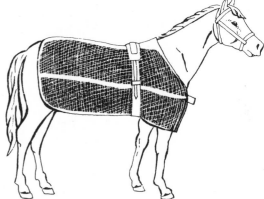

A day rug *is not absolutely essential though it does serve many useful purposes. It is made from wool and is particularly useful when travelling or at shows. Day rugs are made in a variety of colours, and may have the owner's name or monogram marked on them.*

The anti-sweat sheet, *or, as it is sometimes simply called, a sweat sheet, is used to prevent a horse or pony from suddenly becoming chilled after exercise or heavy work. It works on the same principle as a string vest and is used in summer instead of a blanket.*

Shoeing

Younger riders will have heard, read or been told over and over again that the old saying 'no feet, no horse' is still as valid today as it was when first said many years ago. Unless the feet of a horse or pony are sound and well shod, and are properly examined and looked after, the animal cannot be considered in good condition. Neglected feet can completely upset a horse's balance and strain the tendons and ligaments. They will create problems that cannot easily be solved by a vet or by the farrier.

A horse or pony, whether stable-kept or grass-kept, must have his feet checked daily. This does not simply mean seeing that the shoes are not too badly worn or cast (lost) and that the clenches have not risen. It also means checking the condition of the sole of the foot, examining the frog and ensuring that the walls of the hoof are not in bad condition and becoming cracked.

The farrier's advice must always be considered. His job is a very highly skilled one. He has to remove worn shoes, trim the walls of the feet, especially where these have become overgrown, make new shoes, whether by the hot or cold method, fit the shoes to the hooves, and generally ensure that the horse or pony is well shod.

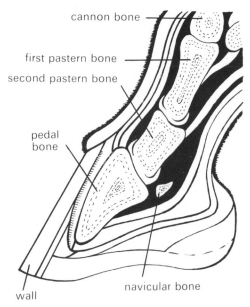

Above: A plan of the foot showing the names given to the joints, bones and other parts. A study of this picture will help young riders to appreciate how complicated a structure the horse's foot is.

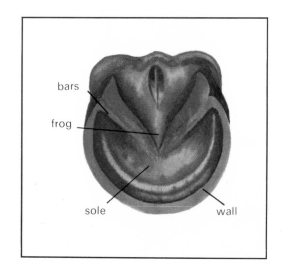

Right: The sole of a foot, showing the frog, bars, sole and wall.

Above: Nowadays there are fewer forges, so a farrier must sometimes serve a very wide area. Many farriers have therefore taken to travelling from one customer to another at regular intervals to shoe their horses or ponies. Most animals need to be re-shod at least every six weeks, and more often if they are working hard.

standard shoe

light racing shoe

shoe for
a draught horse

Left: The type of shoe used will vary according to the horse and the work it is to do. A draught horse needs a heavy shoe for it pulls heavy loads; a race horse has very light shoes that are changed frequently; a riding horse wears medium-weight shoes.

Right: The farrier must
first remove the old shoe
by 'knocking up', or
cutting off, with the end
of his buffer.

Right: Once the buffer
has opened a space, the
pincers are used to pull
the old shoe away.

Far right: When the shoe
has been removed, the
farrier uses a drawing-
knife or 'searcher' to clean
the sole of the foot.

Right: The rasp is used
to smooth down the sole
to enable the new shoe to
fit closely and to allow an
even distribution of
weight to be carried.

Far right: The pritchel
brings the hot shoe from
the forge for scorching.
This is to check whether
or not the shoe fits. A
horse feels no pain or
discomfort when this is
done.

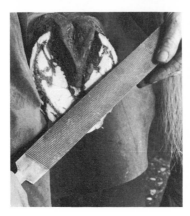

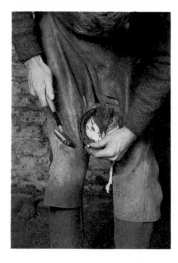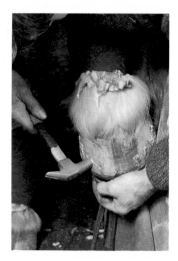

Above: Having made the new shoe, and having checked by scorching that it fits, the farrier begins by nailing on with his driving hammer. He will begin fixing the new shoe with the inside nails, finishing with the nail at the outside of the heel.

Above, left and right: Once the nails have been hammered through the wall, the ends are turned over or 'wrung off' by using the head of the pincers. The clenches are turned over before being tapped into the wall of the foot.

Left: The farrier's tool kit, with a driving hammer, buffer, pincers, a searcher or drawing knife, a toe knife, rasp, nails and leather apron.

The vet

All riders, and the parents of younger riders, should know something of the work so patiently and skilfully carried out by the veterinary surgeon. Years of study are necessary before a veterinary surgeon qualifies. And his (or her) services are available to the owner or rider before a pony is bought, at the time of purchase, and whenever needed afterwards.

Let us look at those three occasions in more detail. First, the vet can give advice about the sort of horse or pony that it would be suitable to buy. He will need to know where the pony will be kept and what kind of grazing or stabling is available. He will also need to know something about the previous experience of those who will be looking after the animal. And, he will want to discuss feeding.

Second, a veterinary suregon's examination before a horse or pony is bought is absolutely essential. He will check the soundness of the animal, its action and its overall state of health. There are certain conditions that cannot be discovered unless an X-ray examination is carried out, and he may recommend this. At the end of his examination, he will prepare a report of his findings.

Third, most ponies at some time or other develop signs of sickness or lameness. Some of these can be treated at home. But if there is doubt, the vet must be called at an early stage.

A first-aid box

In every stable there should be a special place for the medicine cupboard, and a smaller medicine box should be carried in a horse-box or a trailer. The suggested contents for a stable-kept medicine cabinet are: a pair of short, blunt-ended surgical scissors; calico bandages of varying widths; several rolls of cotton wool; lint; a roll or two of gamgee or similar tissue; some packets of oiled silk; a bottle of embrocation; witch hazel; kaolin; one or two colic drinks from the vet (he will advise how long these should be kept before replacing); some dusting powder; Epsom salts; and a bottle of glycerine.

When you use any item from the medicine cupboard or box, be sure to remember to replace it. Otherwise you will be in trouble next time you need it.

This veterinary surgeon watches the pony's movement carefully as it is walked-up in front of him. Lameness, and leg disorders can be detected by this simple exercise, but a trained eye is essential. The ground should be flat and preferably hard so that any defects in the horse's movements can be seen clearly. If a horse is lame its weight will not be evenly distributed when it is walked or trotted; the hind quarters will sink lower on the side of the strong leg.

3 : Saddlery

A saddle and a bridle are the basic items of tack that a horse or pony must have. There are many makes of each to choose from: the important consideration in deciding what to buy is not how smart or how 'fancy' an item looks, but how well it fits the horse and how well it is made. Unfortunately, good leather tack is expensive; but an owner or rider should always buy the best he can afford. Well-made equipment is safer and more comfortable, and will last for many years if properly cared-for. Often, it is more sensible to buy well-made secondhand tack than to buy a new saddle or bridle of inferior quality. But it is essential to examine secondhand equipment carefully to make sure that it has been cleaned regularly and conscientiously maintained. The fact that a few minor repairs are needed does not matter too much – so long as they are dealt with before use.

Having been 'tacked-up' this horse has been tied to the stable wall with a head-collar. A numnah has been placed under the saddle. The stirrups have been 'run up' on the leathers. This must always be done before tacking-up, and no horse or pony should be left at any time with the leathers down and the stirrups loose.

The saddle

The saddle in common use today is very similar to saddles used centuries ago, the basic principle being to keep the weight of the rider from pressing down on the spine of the horse or pony. Even in early times, it was recognized that a saddle that was only a flat pad did not protect a pony from damage. The need to keep the rider from sitting down on the spine led to the introduction of the frame around which saddles are built – the 'tree'.

For long, the saddle tree was made of wood; but wooden trees were heavy and were liable to break if dropped. Today, although wood is still sometimes used, fibreglass, plastics or laminated substances are more common.

The saddler (the craftsman who makes saddles) builds up a saddle from one of three sizes of tree: narrow, medium or wide. His skill is the ability to provide well-fitting saddles of different lengths and widths for all sizes and shapes of horses and ponies.

It seems hardly necessary to say here that a saddle must fit the horse or pony properly. But, only too often, one sees a saddle in use that is too short, too long or too narrow. A badly fitting saddle will cause distress to the pony and can make for an unsafe and uncomfortable ride.

The saddle in general use today is known as an *all-purpose saddle*. It can be used for many equestrian activities, including hacking, hunting and jumping.

Specially designed saddles are required by those who wish to show their ponies to advantage, and for dressage, riding side-saddle and racing.

The *Western saddle*, which is becoming

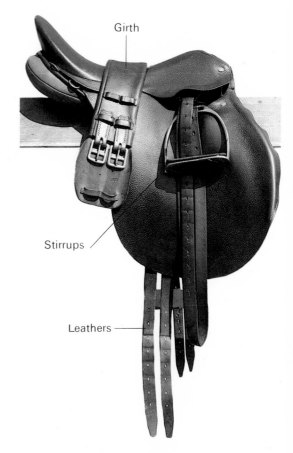

An all-purpose saddle showing leathers, stirrups run up on the leathers and the girth.

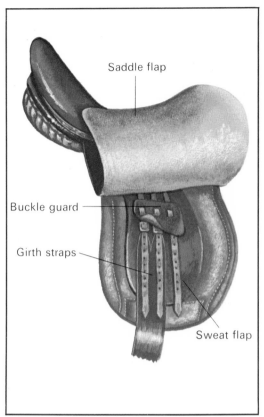

Saddle flap

Buckle guard

Girth straps

Sweat flap

increasingly popular in Europe, originated in the United States. With their individual and elaborate designs, Western saddles are built with a high front and a raised back, giving a comfortable ride for those who spend hours each day on horseback.

Leathers. Stirrup leathers are fitted to the bar on either side of the saddle, and their function is to hold the stirrup irons. Leathers are made from cowhide or rawhide; they tend to stretch with wear.

Stirrup irons. Although nickel plate and other metals are used, the best-quality stirrups are made from stainless steel. They should be wide enough to allow the boots or shoes to go in and out without difficulty. Many different styles of stirrups are available.

Below: The American Western saddle is used for pleasure riding nowadays, although its original and, continuing purpose, is for stock riding and for working with horses and cattle. Magnificent saddles, like this heavily decorated silver saddle, are used in shows and special displays.

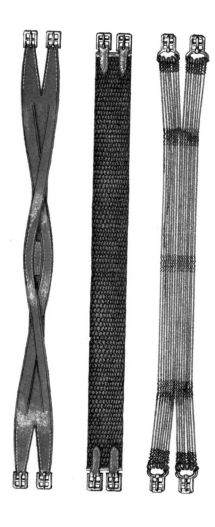

Left: Every saddle must have a girth to hold it in position. Girths can be made from leather, webbing, nylon or a mixture of those materials. The sizes vary from approximately 36 inches (92 cm) for small ponies to 54 inches (1.35 m) for a horse. Here, from left to right; a plaited leather girth; a plain webbing girth; a nylon girth.

When choosing girths, as with all other tack. one has to balance the cost against the other advantages or disadvantages. Leather girths are expensive, but they last longer and they are easier to keep in good condition. Webbing girths, although they are cheaper, are sometimes only considered truly safe when they are used in pairs.

Right: The choice of stirrup irons is largely a matter of personal preference. There is a wide variety of shapes and designs from which to choose. A stirrup iron should be heavy and be a size or so larger than the rider's boot, so that the foot will be quickly released in a fall.

Popular with young riders are the plain hunting iron (1) and the special Simplex safety iron (2) which originated in Australia. This latter iron is shaped on one side to allow the foot to be quickly released in times of emergency. The plain hunting iron is probably the one most commonly used. Also shown are the bent top iron (3) and another version of the hunting iron (4). This one has a rubber tread to give a better grip for the soles of shoes or riding boots.

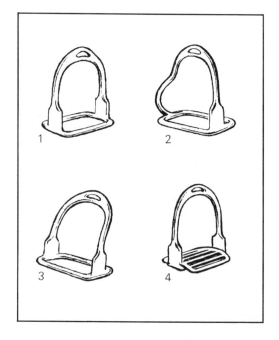

Bridles and bits

The bridle is the piece of equipment that is placed round the horse's head to support the bit. There are five main groups of bridles: the snaffle; the Weymouth or double bridle; the Pelham; the gag; and the Hackamore or bitless bridle.

Of these, the three most commonly used as the *snaffle*, the *Pelham* and the *double bridle*. The other two are for more experienced riders. The snaffle bridle is the one recommended for all novice and younger riders. It is the most gentle of devices, and is far less likely to cause discomfort to a horse than either the Pelham or the double bridle.

Every bridle is made up of the same parts, though they may not all take the same form. The parts are: a headpiece and throat lash (sometimes called a throat-latch), a browband, cheekpieces, a noseband and reins.

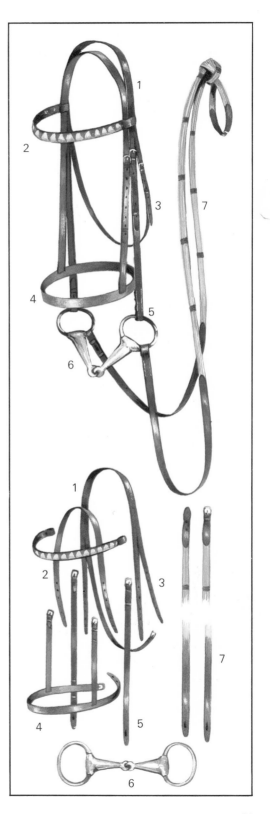

Above: A snaffle bridle with a cavesson noseband. When a bridle is thoroughly cleaned it should be taken to pieces. It is therefore important to recognize the various parts of it for re-assembling. These are shown right: 1 headpiece; 2 browband; 3 throat lash; 4 noseband; 5 cheek pieces; 6 an eggbut snaffle bit; 7 reins.

The double bridle

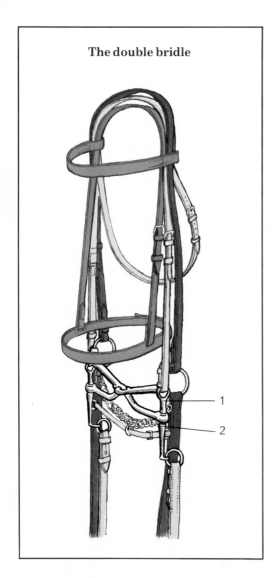

Above: The double bridle, or Weymouth, is a combination of a snaffle-type bitting device used with a curb chain. The bit is specially designed to allow the action of the snaffle (1) to raise the horse's head and the curb chain (2) to bring the head inwards from the poll. This is not a bridle recommended for younger riders. The Pelham which acts in a similar fashion on the horse's head is far more gentle.

The functioning of a bridle

The energy of a horse's forward movement comes from behind the saddle; the bit is the means by which the rider can control it and allow for the various changes of pace and direction. (Though as far as direction is concerned, the legs of the rider should play a more positive part.) Bits operate on a number of different parts of the horse's head; the choice of bit, and the way it is used, demands some appreciation of what happens when the rider takes hold of the reins and begins to apply or loosen pressure.

The snaffle

The snaffle bit is the type most commonly used throughout the world. It is the mildest form of bit, and is used in most equestrian activities. The snaffle can be made from metal, rubber, vulcanite or plastic. It can take the form of a straight bar, or can be jointed to give additional pressure. The bit has a ring at each end to which the single reins of the snaffle bridle are attached. Sometimes, cheekpieces are added, as in the case of the Fulmer or half moon cheek snaffle. Some other snaffles are made with less severe corners to avoid pinching the corners or bars of the mouth.

The Pelham

The Pelham bit, which is also often seen, combines in one mouthpiece the effect of two bits: a snaffle bit and a curb bit. The reins are attached to the rings in the bitting device, which can be made to several different designs.

The Hackamore

The Hackamore, which is now being seen more frequently in the jumping rings, is a bitless bridle demanding skilled hands, a great knowledge of horsemanship and an appreciation of the bad effect it can have if wrongly used. No part of the Hackamore passes through the horse's mouth, but it has metal cheekpieces so shaped that

Understanding the action of all items of saddlery and equipment helps one to appreciate why each item must fit correctly and be secure.

Here the action of the curb chain shows clearly. One can see how painful it would be for the horse or pony if improperly used. To avoid being cruel, make sure that you realize what is happening to the curb chain before pulling too hard on the rein. It is most important to know what happens to the horse or pony when any item of equipment is being badly used or handled.

Below: The mouthpiece of a bit bears upon the bars of the mouth, that is the area of the gum between the molar and incisor teeth.

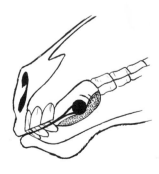

pressure is applied to the nose and chin groove by means of a leather strap. The Hackamore is operated by a single rein.

Choosing and fitting a bit

It will now be seen that a horse is controlled through its mouth and the bitting device used. The bridle, with all its various parts, also plays a part. It cannot be over-emphasized that trying different types of bits in the belief that a horse or pony may 'go better' is a dangerous thing to do. If the pony you are riding has a hard mouth (one that has lost sensitivity, possibly by rough handling) little can be done to put this right. It does not make sense to try a more severe form of bit.

There is, however, an absolute need to ensure that any bit used correctly fits the mouth of the horse or pony. Bits must be neither too small nor too large. And, if a novice is in any doubt about the bit being used, it is only common sense for

him to seek the advice of a rider with experience, a saddler or a veterinary surgeon.

Choosing other parts of a bridle

Reins: Reins, whether plain or plaited, are made of leather, webbing, nylon, string or cotton.

Nosebands are part of the bitting device, and the choice of noseband must depend on the type of bridle and bit being used. A plain Cavesson is always used with a double bridle, and a special type of Cavesson is always used when lungeing. Other nosebands are the dropped noseband, which is made in several patterns and which is used with a snaffle; the flash noseband (a form of Cavesson with two straps that cross and are fastened below the bit); and the grackle.

Nosebands are all designed for special purposes; so you need advice to choose one.

The curved or straight bit is the gentlest type, particularly when made of rubber. It is used for young horses with sensitive mouths. The single-jointed bit, like the eggbutt snaffle, exerts more pressure. The Kimblewick is a severe bit, only to be used by those who really understand its effect. The Pelham combines the action of a snaffle and curb bit in one. The Weymouth has a curb chain and is used with a separate snaffle (a bridoon). The bridles for both these bits have double reins.

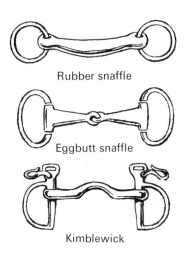

Rubber snaffle

Eggbutt snaffle

Kimblewick

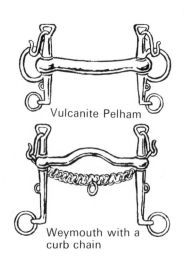

Vulcanite Pelham

Weymouth with a curb chain

Right: A hackamore is a bitless bridle—that is, it has no mouthpiece. But it is a very severe form of bitting device, exerting pressure as it does on the nose and chin groove.

Below: In America, the 'flat' saddle with its very low seat is used for show jumping. This show Hunter has a full-cheek snaffle and a breast-plate with no martingale. Its mane, forelock and tail are plaited.

Protective clothing

In addition to saddles, bridles and other items necessary for riding a horse or pony, every stable requires miscellaneous items of equipment, some of which might come under a general heading of 'protective clothing'.

First, however, is the headcollar, an item used perhaps more frequently than any other piece of equipment. In the long run it is cheaper to buy the best available. It is worth repeating that one should never try to save money by buying cheaply made items. Look for brass fittings, especially the small square fitting through which a rope with a safety hook is fastened. This rope is used both to lead a horse or pony and to tie him up.

Buckets, skips or baskets, forks, shovels and brooms are all part of stable equipment. They are the tools required to keep the stable clean, tidy and hygienic. Protective clothing includes rugs (dealt with separately) and bandages (for exercising and travelling, and tail bandages), fetlock boots, over-reach boots, brushing boots, tail guards and knee caps.

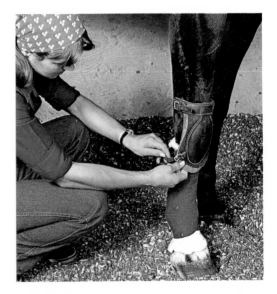

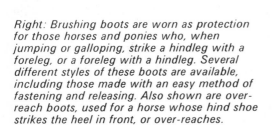

Right: Brushing boots are worn as protection for those horses and ponies who, when jumping or galloping, strike a hindleg with a foreleg, or a foreleg with a hindleg. Several different styles of these boots are available, including those made with an easy method of fastening and releasing. Also shown are over-reach boots, used for a horse whose hind shoe strikes the heel in front, or over-reaches.

Right: A horse prepared for travelling with a tail guard neatly fixed.

Left: When travelling, horses' or ponies' knees are particularly liable to knocks. The best form of protection is to use kneecaps, sometimes called kneeguards. Many varieties are available, the best having a circle of leather sewn over the area of the knee. You should not tighten the lower strap. It will restrict movement and causes rubbing if you do.

Below: Bandages protect the legs against injury and provide some support for the tendons.

To fix a bandage, first place some gamgee, cotton wool or tissue around the leg. Next, take the rolled-up bandage and wrap round the leg, working neatly from the knee to the coronet and back again towards the starting point. The tapes are tied and the ends tucked securely into the folds.

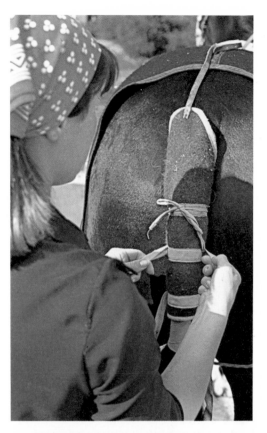

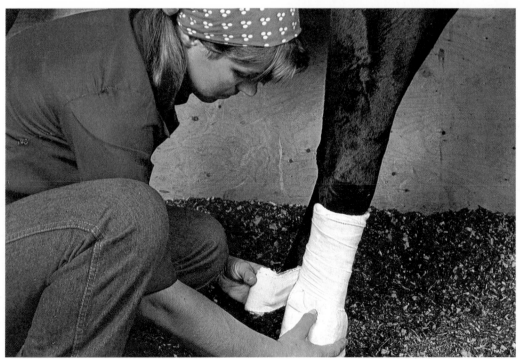

Tacking up

Above: The correct way to carry a saddle, with the bridle across the shoulder. In this way, one arm remains free.

Putting on a saddle

A horse or pony should be tied up to the stable door or a secure post before being saddled. Tacking up is quite complicated, and the last thing the rider wants is to have to go and search for a missing item of tack leaving the pony standing free, and likely to wander off. In any case, it is much safer to have him tied up.

Approach the near side of the pony with the saddle carried over your right arm. The girth should hang over the seat of the saddle. The stirrups should be 'run up' on the leathers, so they do not flap about and hit the horse or pony. Talk to the pony and give him a reassuring pat. Place the saddle high on the withers, and slowly slide it into the correct position. This avoids the hairs being rubbed the wrong way.

Having seen that the saddle looks correct from the near side, go round and check the off side, making sure that all is tidy. Check that the sweat flaps and saddle flaps are lying straight and have not been turned over. Release the girth, which will have been hanging over the saddle, and allow it to hang down.

Return to the near side and fasten the girth, but not too tightly. The tension should be such that the saddle will not slip when you pull yourself up when mounting, but not so tight that it causes discomfort. The stirrups will be run down the leathers just before mounting and adjusted when the rider is in the saddle.

If you are using a martingale, this will have to be fixed, of course, before the girth is buckled up.

Taking off a saddle

A pony should be tied up to be unsaddled, just as to be saddled. However, he probably will already have been tied up anyway to have his bridle taken off.

The first jobs are to run up the stirrups and release the girth buckles on the near side. Allow the girth to hang loosely: it will fall to the off side.

Move to the off side and place the girth across the seat of the saddle. Then return to the near side and gently lift the saddle off the pony's back. Put it on a saddle rack or tree, though it will require cleaning before it is put away.

It is kind to the pony always to release some of the tension around his belly when you dismount. Releasing the girth by one or two holes makes quite a difference to him. But never forget to check the girth before remounting.

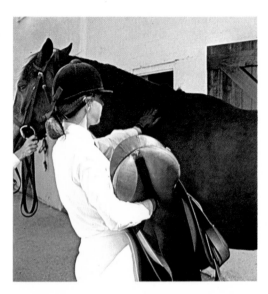

Be sure the horse or pony is tied-up or held before starting to saddle-up. Approach the horse or pony from the near-side. Give a reassuring pat.

Place the saddle on gently and well forward onto the withers. Carefully slide it backwards into position, making certain that the hairs are smoothed before fastening.

Bring the girth through from the far side.

Tighten the girth, which will be adjusted again after mounting.

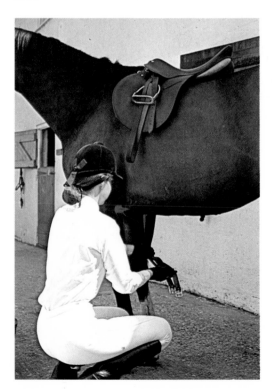

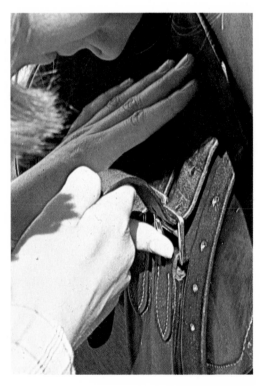

Putting on a bridle

Most riders begin to tack up from the near side, though when putting on a bridle or saddle you will have to move to the front and to the off side before all the necessary adjustments can be made.

The headcollar, which should have been tied with a quick release knot to a loop of string attached to the stable door or a firm post, must be removed and buckled around the pony's neck before attempting to introduce the bridle. Some ponies willingly accept the bit and stand still while being tacked up. Others tend to become excitable, which is why the headcollar should not be removed completely. Carrying the bridle by placing it over one shoulder will allow you to have both hands and arms free to deal with the headcollar. Remember to put the reins over the pony's head and neck, and have one arm through them before releasing the headcollar. By doing so, you will have some control should the pony make any move.

Above right: Before beginning to put on the bridle, see that the horse or pony is tied up. This should preferably be done with a headcollar or halter loosely tied around the neck. Pass the reins over the horse's head and down onto his neck. Holding the headpiece in the right hand, take the bit in the left hand. Using the fingers to open the mouth at the side (where there are no teeth) and guide the bit into the horse's mouth without knocking the teeth.

Right: Draw the bridle up and pass the headpiece over each ear. Pull the forelock out over the brow band. Check that the bit is now in the right position.

Left: Begin now to tighten the buckles, starting with the noseband and the throat lash. The buckles will not be completed until the correct positioning of the bridle has been checked. To fit comfortably the nose band should allow two fingers between it and the horse or pony's jawbone.

Left: Having seen that the bridle is straight, and the only way this can be checked is to move to the front of the horse, return to complete the tightening of the straps, ensuring that the end of each strap is placed into its 'keeper'. No strap should be too tight. The space between the head and throat lash can be measured by seeing that three fingers' space has been allowed.

Taking off a bridle

Before starting to remove a pony's bridle, make sure that you have a headcollar ready to put on, preferably one already fixed to a ring on a wall or post. Horses and ponies, when they return from exercise or a ride, do not always settle down quickly. Not infrequently, a pony will attempt to 'take-off' once he is free from the bridle–even though he is in his own stable yard.

If you fix a headcollar around his neck while the bridle is being removed, you will have a means of controlling him.

When the buckles of the noseband and

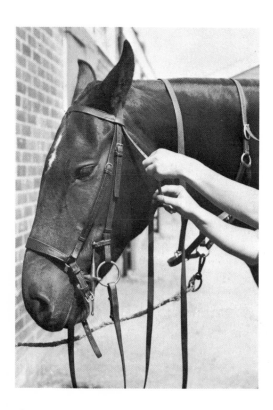

Above: Before taking off the bridle, a halter or headcollar is fastened loosely around the neck of the horse. Put the reins over the horse's neck. Standing on the nearside begin removing the bridle by undoing the throat lash and noseband.

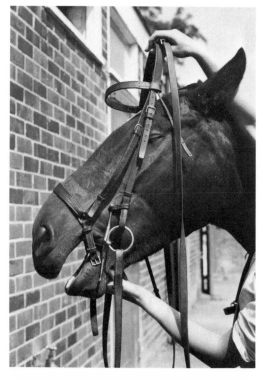

Above: When the straps are undone, have the left hand ready to receive the bit and gently lift the headpiece over the ears. Allow the bridle to come down over the horse's face. The left hand will then take the bit. Never force the bit from the horse or pony's mouth.

throat lash, and the curb chain if one has been used, are unhooked, the bridle should be held as the illustration shows. Slip the headpiece over the ears, and have your left hand placed ready to receive the bit. Allow the bridle to come slightly away from the pony's head. Once the headpiece has been removed, the pony will release the bit, and the complete bridle will come over and into your left hand. It can then be hung over the shoulder.

The headcollar is now transferred to its correct position and buckled.
Some riders like to have a headcollar fitted to a horse or pony when it is being grazed. This makes a 'difficult' animal much easier to catch. Where a headcollar has been fitted, the approach should be cautious. It is quite surprising how quickly a pony will learn that the sight of a rope means he is to be taken away from his grazing! Keep the rope behind your back, or out of sight, having the safety clip ready for fastening as you reach the pony.

Below: There are many uses for a headcollar or halter; younger riders should recognize early in their riding life the essential part they both play in stable management. A halter is a type of headcollar made from strong webbing.

Above: Once the bridle has been removed, it should again be hung over a shoulder, and never dropped on the ground. Then the headcollar is put on. The horse or pony is now ready for putting out into a field or being led into its stable.

Care of saddlery

Well-fitting tack that has been properly maintained gives a pony a smart appearance and – more important – is essential to the safety of the rider. It is for this reason that we emphasize the necessity for cleaning tack each time it has been used. Never put any tack away until it has been cleaned and examined.

Leather requires constant oiling to prevent it becoming dry and cracked. New tack must be treated with a lubricant to soften the leather and make it more pliable. When cleaning tack, you must do more than simply remove mud or dirt. You must take the opportunity to examine it for wear and damage. Check that the stitching is not broken or becoming worn, and that the buckles are not damaged and unsafe.

Cleaning the saddle

The equipment needed for cleaning tack is: a bucket of clean water, saddle soap, a tin of metal polish to be used on the buckles and stirrup irons, two sponges, a soft leather for drying, clean dusters, and a brush for cleaning the linings of the saddle.

First remove the girth and stirrup leathers. Then stand the saddle on its pommel or, preferably, put it across a saddle horse. Wash the leather with a

With saddlery being so expensive to buy, there is every incentive to keep it in good condition. It is also of benefit to the horse or pony that all tack is clean. Here, two saddles are being cleaned across a saddle 'horse'.

dampened sponge, removing all dirt. Next apply the saddle soap, again by using a dampened sponge, and work it well into the leather. Do not have the sponge too wet, and do not use too much saddle soap. While washing and soaping, make sure that no excess water reaches the lining of the saddle.

Before the saddle is polished, it should again be sponged down to remove surplus soap and then dried with the soft leather. The girth and stirrups must not be overlooked. If the stirrup irons have rubber treads, they should be removed before cleaning. And the metal should be washed and dried before metal polish is used.

When the saddle has been thoroughly and carefully polished, it is reassembled and put away in the tack room. Cover it with a clean duster or stable rubber.

Cleaning the bridle

Cleaning the bridle is a little more in-volved, though perhaps not such hard work. First, it is necessary to undo all the buckles and separate the leather straps that make up the bridle. Each strap is then washed and treated with soap exactly as was done with the saddle. When all is dry, and each buckle has been polished, the bridle is reassembled before being 'put up' in the correct manner.

Remember that tack will be safer, more comfortable and smarter, and will last longer if kept clean and well cared for.

Below: One of the more important jobs is to keep the tack room clean and tidy. Saddles, as shown, should be on racks, and bridles properly run-up and hung. No tack should ever be put away in a dirty state. This tack room is neat and clean; the signs of a well-run and experienced stable.

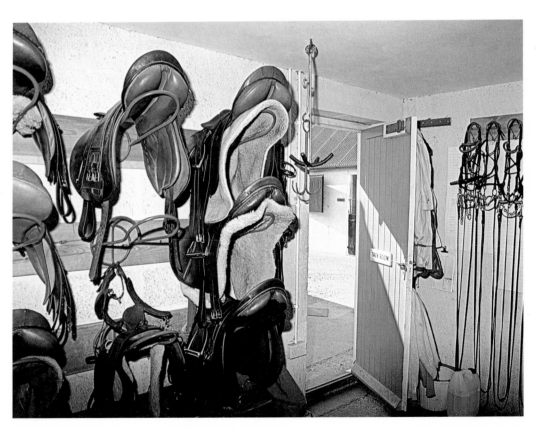

4: Learning to ride

A good horseman or horsewoman appears to ride effortlessly, doing all the right things without even having to think about them. Horse and rider work together with complete understanding, each seeming to anticipate the wishes and movements of the other. This harmony has to be learnt. The rider has to know how a horse or pony thinks and how he can be encouraged to give of his best. This calls for sympathy and for clear communication by means of the aids—the rider's hands, seat, legs, and voice being used with skill to tell the horse exactly what is needed of him. And the horse must have learnt how to interpret the aids without any misunderstanding, and how to use his great strength and agility to best advantage.

Right: Two young riders returning from a ride, one wearing a black riding coat, the other a hacking jacket. Both wear hard hats, a rule of sensible horsemanship. Horses and ponies enjoy the company of other animals when exercising. A young or nervous horse can be helped by the example of a steadier more experienced one.

What to wear when riding

Before mounting, make sure that you are wearing sensible clothes that give proper protection. Never get on a horse or pony unless you are wearing a hard riding hat. A jacket, anorak or long-sleeved jumper or sweater will protect your arms and body, and trousers or jeans will protect your legs. The boots or shoes that you wear should have heels deep enough to stop your feet sliding through the stirrup irons. You should not, however, wear high heels when riding. Sometimes, special riding clothes are necessary; for example, in certain competitions at horse shows. But for ordinary exercising and hacking, the most important considerations are safety and comfort. A hard hat is essential at all times when riding; in fact, it is recommended that a hard hat be worn by younger and novice riders even when working around a stable or attending to a pony in a field.

Although safety is the prime consideration, smartness is important, too. You should always try to look neat and tidy. Even a well-cared-for pony looks bad when being ridden by a slovenly dressed rider.

Mounting

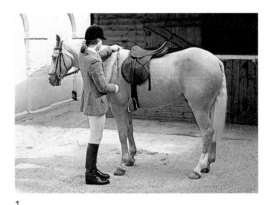

1

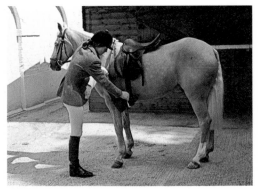

2

1: When mounting, approach from the near (left) side. Stand with the left shoulder to the horse, and the reins in the left hand. Place the left hand with the reins, onto the withers.

2: Hold the nearside leather with the right hand and place the left foot into the stirrup, still retaining hold with the left hand.

3: Take hold of the cantle of the saddle with the right hand and raise the body. The left toe will now be pointing to the nearside of the horse. Throw the right leg over the quarters.

4: Settle quietly and gently into the saddle, taking up the reins with both hands. Place the right foot into the stirrup iron and sit still until ready to move off.

Among the early lessons given to a young horse when it is being trained is that it should stand square and still when at the halt.

However, many ponies, once preparations for a ride begin, are only too anxious to move off. They fidget around and will not stand still. If the pony you ride is like this, you must spend time in teaching him to be patient–especially at the moment of mounting.

You should approach from the near side with your shoulder almost touching the pony's near (left) shoulder. Take hold of the reins and give a reassuring pat. Rest your left hand, still holding the reins, firmly on the front of the withers. It is a good idea for younger riders to grasp the mane with the left hand. Taking the stirrup with your right hand, place your left foot into the iron. Then, pressing your toes under the girth, swing your body round until you are facing the pony side-on. Your right hand is now placed firmly on the back of the waist of the saddle, and with a spring you swing your right leg over the quarters–making sure that you

3

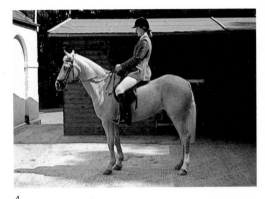

4

do not kick the pony! Your right hand is moved from the waist of the saddle to the front arch to allow you to come quietly into a sitting position. Then you place your right foot in the iron and take the reins up with both hands.

Now sit still for a moment. Make sure that the leathers are at the correct length; if not, shorten or lengthen them as necessary by means of the buckles.

You must also now adjust the girth. First, take both reins in the right hand. Move your left knee and leg forward to make the saddle flap and buckle guard accessible. Lift these and tighten the girth as necessary. When satisfied, let the buckle guard and saddle flap go back to their normal position.

The reins should now once again be taken up in both hands.

Right: Once mounted the rider should tighten the girth. To do this move the left leg forward and lift the saddle flap. Take hold of the girth strap and use the forefinger to guide the pin of the buckle into the strap.

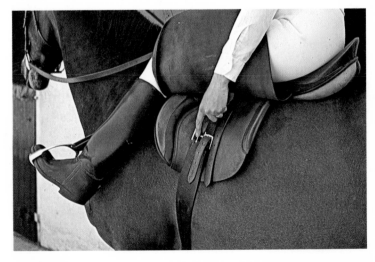

Dismounting

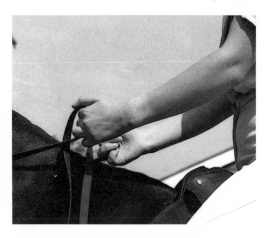

Above: When the rider is mounted and has tightened the girth, the reins are taken up in both hands as shown here. You are then ready to move off.

When dismounting, make sure the pony stands till and square. Take both reins into the left hand. Remove both feet from the stirrups and lean slightly forward. Then place your left hand, still holding the reins, on the pony's neck and your right hand on the pommel of the saddle. With a gentle and smooth push, swing your right leg back over the quarters to the near side, and land on your toes standing facing the saddle. Move along to the pony's head and you are ready to lead him away.

Three points are particularly worth noting. These are:

Never have the feet in the stirrup irons while dismounting. If you do, and the pony moves off, you may easily have an awkward accident.

Never grasp the reins so tightly that the pony will feel a jab in its mouth.

Never try to dismount by bringing the right leg over the front of the saddle and sliding off. You cannot do so while retaining hold of the reins and therefore being in control of the horse or pony.

Aids to Mounting

In some situations mounting can be a problem. A large horse may be a daunting sight to a child or adult who is not very tall and anyone lacking the agility to spring astride with ease. There are several ways of making the task of mounting easier.

If another pair of hands is available, a 'leg-up' is the answer. The rider stands in the mounting position with his left leg bent. The helper holds the rider's left knee and by pushing upwards gives him the spring necessary to get him into the saddle.

Some stables have concrete mounting blocks in the stable yard. By standing on the block the distance between the rider and the saddle is greatly decreased.

If a rider has to dismount when out hacking and has trouble remounting, he should look for a convenient tree stump to use as an improvised mounting block.

Another aid to mounting is the adjustable stirrup leather. A length of webbing or canvas is inserted into the near side leather. This gives an extra-long leather — making mounting much easier. When the rider is in the saddle the extra length of canvas is hooked up, and the stirrup leather is then the normal length.

Above: When dismounting the horse should be standing quietly and square to the ground. First remove both feet from the stirrups. Put the reins in the left hand on the horse's neck.

Above: Keeping hold of the reins in the left hand, place the right hand on the pommel of the saddle. Swing the right leg cleanly over the hindquarters.

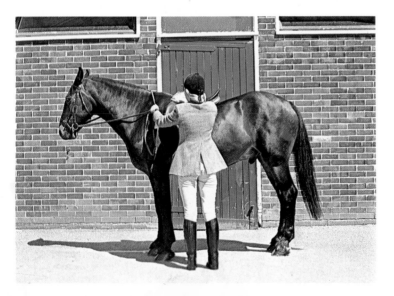

Left: The dismounting action is one of vaulting. On landing the toes of both feet should come down first; the rider should land facing the nearside of the horse or pony.

The aids

Aids are the signals by which the rider tells the horse or pony what to do. They are a form of language between rider and pony, and fall into two groups. The *natural aids* are signals given by the use of the rider's body seat, legs, voice and hands. The body and seat aids are given by altering the position and pressure of the body. The leg aids are conveyed by pressure against the horse's sides. And the hand aids control the horse's head through the reins and bit. The voice is used for encouraging and disciplining. The *artificial aids* are signals given by means of a whip or stick, martingale or spurs.

The natural aids

The natural aids are used in conjunction with each other, the rider employing legs, seat, voice and hands in a way that effectively conveys his wishes to the horse or pony. But, of course, the meaning of the aids has to be understood by both rider and horse. They produce results only with horses and ponies that have been trained to understand their meaning. They will not work on young or untrained animals, and they will not work unless they are given correctly.

In the first practical lessons a novice has, the aids are explained. But it takes time and practice to make the aids 'come together'. Similarly, it takes time for a pony to understand all that is being asked of him.

Ideally, the rider seeks an immediate response from the pony when the aids are applied; but this may not be easy to achieve if the pony is young or unused to his rider. A young pony should have the aids given with a slight over-emphasis. But, to get the best results, the aids should always be the lightest that are possible in the particular circumstances.

Right: The legs are the aids used to create and continue forward movement of the horse. They are also used to control the horse's hindquarters. The legs should be held steady at the girth except when giving a signal, so that the horse is not confused by continual bumping. The foot should not move back too far from this position or it will only annoy the horse.

Left: The natural aids are: the voice (to praise, reprimand or give an order); the hands (to control and communicate through the bit); the legs (to signal the movement); the seat (to follow the horse's movements from a central position).

Left: When a whip, one of the artificial aids, is carried, the correct position for it is to lie back across the rider's thigh, as here.

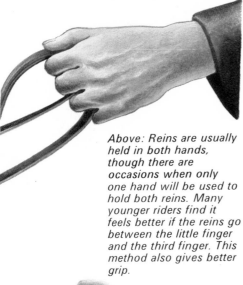

Above: Reins are usually held in both hands, though there are occasions when only one hand will be used to hold both reins. Many younger riders find it feels better if the reins go between the little finger and the third finger. This method also gives better grip.

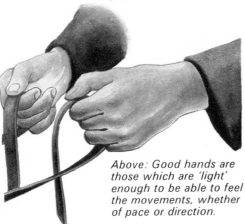

Above: Good hands are those which are 'light' enough to be able to feel the movements, whether of pace or direction.

Right: To turn a horse or pony to the left on the forehand from the halt, the rider must first prevent him from moving forward by having a firm feeling on the bit (through the hands) and, at the same time, asking by additional pressure on the left rein that he turn his head slightly towards the left. With the weight of the body central, the left leg is applied behind the girth so as to move the horse's quarters to the right. At this time, the rider should keep his right leg close to the girth to stop the horse from attempting to move backwards.

When this movement is correctly carried out the near-fore of the horse or pony will become a pivot around which he will turn. Once a turn has been started, and a few steps taken, the horse should be asked to move forward without delay.

When turning to the right these actions are reversed.

Use of the Hands

A good rider is said to have 'good hands' or 'light hands', meaning that he always has sensitive contact with his horse or pony through the reins and bit. Usually, the hands are kept quiet and relaxed, just 'feeling' the horse's mouth, even when it is necessary to allow for movements of the horse's head. In the walk, for example, the horse moves his head up and down, and the rider must keep his elbow joints loose so that his hands can follow this movement while maintaining a light and even contact.

Sometimes, the rider's hands yield slightly–for example, when the horse is being instructed to increase speed. Or they may resist slightly, as when a downward transition of pace is desired or the horse is being told to decrease speed. But the hands must never pull, must never be tense, and must not be allowed to alter their contact because of movements of the rider's body.

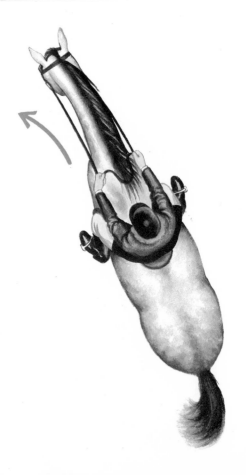

The martingale

Martingales are fitted to keep the pony's head from being thrown upwards. If a young horse or pony has been properly schooled, he is unlikely to need a martingale, but not all ponies have a perfect head carriage. The two most commonly used are the standing martingale and the running martingale.

The standing martingale, attached from the girth of a cavesson noseband, is not recommended for novice owners or riders.

The running martingale is used to keep the reins down so that the bit will work on the bars of the mouth. Like the standing martingale, the running martingale is fitted from the girth; it has two rings at the other end through which the reins are passed. Where this martingale is used with a double bridle, the snaffle rein is the one that goes through the rings.

Other types of martingales are the bib martingale, the Market Harborough and the Irish rings.

Left: A running martingale showing the reins passing through the two rings.

The paces

Horses and ponies have four natural paces or gaits: walk, trot, canter and gallop. At each pace, there is a particular number of steps to each stride. At the walk there are four steps; at the trot, two steps; at the canter, three steps; and at the gallop, four steps.

Moving smoothly from one pace to another (called making a *transition*) is achieved by means of the aids. The horse or pony should make an immediate response.

Young riders may find it difficult to maintain a pace for any length of time: some ponies have a tendency to decide pace for themselves. This is wrong, and must not be allowed. The rider must at all times be the one in control. If a pony, without being asked, makes a transition (change) from one pace to another, he should be brought back quietly to the correct pace; and this should then be maintained for a while.

Moving into and back from the gaits

One of the hardest riding skills to master is to be able to move quickly into, and back from, the four paces. A rider can improve in ability by using the aids, appreciating the ability of the horse or pony, recognizing his or her own skill and experience and being patient and receptive to all lessons and periods of instruction. The knowledge acquired when first being taught to ride will always prove invaluable. But that knowledge will only be of real benefit when continually applied. It is important always to practise as frequently as possible, but never to the point of making the horse or pony bored.

The walk

After being mounted, the horse or pony should be standing still and square, with its weight evenly distributed over each of its legs. The rider's hands should be maintaining a light contact with the pony's mouth. The rider sits deep into the saddle, keeping his back straight but relaxed. His knees and thighs should remain close to the saddle with the lower part of his legs resting quietly against the horse's sides.

In the stirrups, the balls of the rider's feet should lie against the bars. The heels should be lower than the toes, though not too much so.

When all is set, the rider 'asks' the pony to move forward by taking both legs back behind the girth and squeezing them

Walking

Below: The walk *is a pace with a positive stride pattern in which the legs of the horse follow each other in an even rhythm. This pace is not the easiest to*

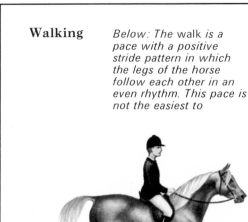

Above: A rider keeping her horse alert at the walk.

maintain, although to be able to keep a horse or pony at an even walking pace is essential.

The four types or styles of walk recognized are the ordinary, collected, extended *and* free. *Each should be* practised and used during periods of exercising and schooling. At the walk, whether leaving the stable yard or out across country, remember the part the rider plays in ensuring the overall effect is pleasing. Never permit yourself to be slovenly; both horse and rider should be alert.

against the pony's sides. It is not correct to start with a series of kicks! The rider's spine is braced and inclined slightly forward. His hands are allowed to 'open', giving the horse or pony room to move forward. It is essential to remember that the hands control the impulsion built up by use of the body, seat and legs. Without 'good' hands it is not possible to have an obedient and controlled forward movement. The pony should maintain the walking pace all the time the correct aid is being applied.

To return to the halt from the walk, the rider sits deeper into the saddle, braces his spine and brings his legs forward slightly, keeping an even pressure against the pony's sides. He 'closes' his hands to the position of light contact with the pony's mouth. The resistence felt by the horse or pony through the action of the rider's hands will be sufficient to bring him back to a halt, but only if the rider's body, seat and legs are functioning as they should be. At the halt, the pony should again stand quietly and square.

The Trot

When changing from a walk to a trot, the aids are as for moving from the halt to the walk. The legs squeeze harder, and the hands, though the reins may be somewhat shorter, remain still and in the correct position. The rider's body moves slightly forward with the change of pace. For many, the trot is the most comfortable of all the four paces. It can be ridden in a sitting or rising position. The sitting trot is used before asking a horse or pony to come back to a walk or to move into a canter.

In the sitting trot, the seat remains in the saddle. In the rising trot the rider rises rhythmically from the saddle in time with the two-beat stride, where the diagonally-opposite legs of the horse or pony move simultaneously.

Words for learners
These are some of the words that a learner will meet with during periods of instruction.

Collected: A 'collected' pace is more controlled with a shorter stride than a normal or 'free' pace.

Collection: A horse or pony is said to be 'collected' when he is ready to carry out his rider's instructions, given through the aids.

Extended: In an 'extended' pace the horse strides out, but must not hurry or lose the regular rhythm of the pace.

Impulsion: The term used for the energy that drives a horse forward. Impulsion comes from behind the saddle in the horse's hindquarters.

Transition: The change or transition from one pace to another either upwards (increasing speed) or downwards (decreasing speed) should always be carried out smoothly.

Trotting

Below: The rider does not alter his body position in moving from a walk to a trot. Do not lean forward. Keep the legs quiet and close to the horse's sides. Should the horse appear anxious to move on, he should be brought back to the rider by shortening the reins.

There are two ways of riding a trot: 'rising' and 'sitting'. In the rising trot, the rider rises up from the saddle and then comes back again in time with the two-beat rhythm of the pace. This is the usual way to ride at a trot, though the sitting trot will be used when making the transition from one pace to another—in other words, when moving from the trot to a canter, or from a trot to the walk. A sitting trot brings the rider into closer contact with his horse or pony.

Although the rising trot may sound easy to achieve it only becomes effective when performed without the rider completely relying on the stirrups. The action of the rising trot should mean using the grip obtained from the knees and thighs. In slowing down, first bring the horse back to a walk, before asking him to halt.

The Canter

The transition from the trot to the canter will again involve the rider in some quiet but positive changes of position. It is made from the sitting trot. The rider increases the pressure applied through the legs, and brings them slightly farther back from the girth. He sits deep into the saddle, and is prepared to allow his body to bend to a forward position. This enables him to 'give' the horse or pony more rein, though without losing the control of the bit.

At the canter, the rider's seat must keep close contact with the saddle. His body position, together with the more definite leg action, will help the transition from the trot and must be maintained throughout the canter. Too many riders are literally thrown out of the saddle the moment the horse changes pace. When this happens, it can mean one of two things: either that the nads have allowed too much rein, or that the body is not sufficiently relaxed. The canter is a far more complicated pace than the walk, the trot or the gallop. The three-beat stride is not easy to master. But every rider knows the joy of moving through the walk and trot and into the canter, which, though not easy, is the most satisfying pace when done well.

Should a horse or pony be given the wrong aids at the moment of change of pace, or if for any reason he has been thrown off balance, even for the briefest moment, he may become 'disunited'. This word describes an error in the sequence of the pace. He can still go forward, but his movement looks wrong and is quite uncomfortable.

The Gallop

The gallop is the fastest pace of a horse or pony and is not a pace for a young or novice rider.

In the gallop, the rider's seat is out of the saddle as he or she leans forward. The stirrups take most of the rider's

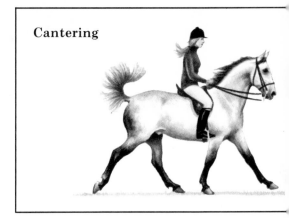

Cantering

The canter is a pace in which the horse or pony moves with a free and natural balance. The horse should be straight from head to tail, and the stride is held in an evenly-accomplished pace. Whether riding an ordinary, collected or extended canter, there is a need to keep up impulsion; a slackening of the forward movement will not allow the horse to move freely. At a collected canter the horse must be supple, though possibly not as active as at an extended canter. The use of the collected and extended strides will be critical when jumping or competing at dressage.

weight, though ideally the knees should play their part.

With the lengthening of the stride and the speed of the pace, it is easy for an inexperienced rider to lose control. It is far more valuable for a younger rider to establish a good, rhythmic canter, or an extended canter, than to gallop and not be able to retain command of his or her mount.

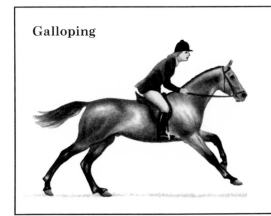

Galloping

The canter is perhaps the most enjoyable and flowing of all a horse's gaits or paces.

Below: At the gallop the rider is in a forward position with the body weight taken on the knees and stirrups. All four feet come well off the ground in the gallop, and the stride is longer than in the canter.

5 : Exercising and schooling

Exercising and schooling have different functions, though many young riders believe that if they are doing one they are doing both. Exercise is essential if a horse or pony is to remain fit or build up his strength, and it enables him to work off surplus energy. Almost as important, it gives both pony and rider an opportunity to get to know and understand each other better, and to practise the skills they have learnt during schooling sessions.

The daily exercise periods should be planned to give pleasure. They should

never be just another job to be tackled. That would be a completely wrong approach; because exercising, apart from the good it does to the fitness and well-being of the horse or pony, is a time when pony and rider can learn something extra about each other. It should be a fun period, combined with some seriousness, if true benefits are to be achieved.

Each occasion when a horse or pony is taken out for a ride should form part of a planned exercise programme. It is not enough to hack over fields or commons or walk along the roads unless some thought has been given to the value and pleasure the ride should give to horse and rider.

Riding on the roads is a useful form of exercise, provided that it is done purposefully. It can be very effective as a means of muscling-up a horse or pony. And if the animal is allowed to walk 'free' for a while so that his mouth is not restricted, he will learn that the moment the rider takes up the reins and brings him back to the bit, he must respond. He must act immediately on the aid he is given.

At exercise the rider, too, must gain something. He can use the period for assessing the standard of his own riding. How balanced is he, and, more important, how balanced is the horse or pony? At opportune moments, perhaps when on a bridle path or a flat area of commonland, the horse or pony can be brought back to a halt and then asked to move on quietly through the paces. He should be taught at exercise to be responsive; but the rider must be sure that he is always given the correct aids.

It is best to exercise with a small group if this is possible. Horses and ponies enjoy company, and two or three moving out together can have a more fruitful and pleasurable time than one on his own.

Schooling

The purpose of schooling is to teach. The most effective way of teaching a horse or pony is to give one short lesson at a time. Trying to teach too many things at the same time only creates boredom.

Some horses and ponies appear slow to learn, but once a horse or pony comes to understand what is being asked, he seldom forgets. This can be a disadvantage if he has been badly taught.

For example, if a pony will not stand still at the halt, especially before being mounted or dismounted, the task facing the rider is to take him back to the beginning and start over again. The pony,

Below: Schooling is a period during which a pony and rider should learn more about each other. Both should be alert and no slackness should be tolerated.

perhaps, was never reprimanded for moving off when the rider took the stirrup to mount. Now, he believes that this is the moment to move.

Schooling can take place in a riding school, in an outdoor manège or in the corner of a paddock. For simple schooling, even the stable yard can be used.

Riding schools

Riding schools have one big advantage in that they have instructors to teach. But beware! Riding schools are not all equally efficient. Some have instructors who are qualified to teach; others use people who, though perhaps excellent riders, do not have the skill to pass on their knowledge and experience. Though schooling is something to be taken quietly, it is most effective when younger riders have someone with experience on the ground to point out errors and to encourage.

A novice's early days are critical. The first lessons teach the basic sitting position, exercises to increase suppleness, and the aids to impart to the horse or pony to allow him to move through the paces. They instil confidence–to my mind the most important lesson of all.

The manège

To improve the balance and obedience of a pony, it is useful to school in a manège, whether this is in a corner of a field or inside a closed area. A manège can be constructed by using two sides of a field and closing the other two with rope or with bales of straw. The outside measurements of such a manège should be 40 metres (44 yards) by 20 metres (22 yards). One advantage of schooling in this confined space is that the horse or pony can be ridden on both left and right reins, and can follow various schooling movements. He can be asked to turn full circles, can weave a serpentine through the middle of the longer side, and can extend or collect across the diagonals.

The diagram below shows some of the movements which can be achieved in a manège prepared to an area of, say 40×20 metres (44×22 yards). It will be seen that the larger circles take up half the width and will have a 10 metres (11 yards) diameter. Other figures are the smaller, tighter circle, figures of eight, different laterals and diagonals, and the use of the extreme outer perimeter track.

Schooling sessions

At all school sessions, each of which should be short, the rider must know what he or she is setting out to achieve. A programme of schooling, planned for a two or three month period at a time, should be followed.

During schooling, neither pony nor rider should be allowed to become lazy or casual in movement or response. The rider must use the aids correctly and never ask the pony for more than can be given.

Lungeing

One of the most useful of all aids used in schooling is the lunge, but this requires skilled hands if it is to be effective. Properly used, the lunge will teach obedience, encourage a free forward movement at different paces, help to develop muscles and suppleness, and improve the balance of the horse or pony.

The lunge rein, made of webbing, is fixed to a special Cavesson noseband. The trainer stands and allows the lunge rein to extend to the required length. The horse or pony is then encouraged by word, and by being *shown* the lunge whip, to move in a circle on either rein.

In addition to the movements which can be practised in a manege, it is always useful to have a horse or pony going quietly before any set routine or exercise. Here, walking through a line of coloured poles, placed at measured distances from one another, helps the pony and rider to work towards this objective.

6 : Jumping

The world-wide interest in show jumping is shared by people of all ages. Through television, millions have an opportunity to watch top-class horses and riders showing their skill in national and international competitions. And the hundreds of thousands of people who visit the many horse shows staged throughout the world particularly enjoy the jumping competitions.

All who ride, whether competitively or not, know the thrill and excitement of asking their horse or pony to jump. Younger riders, and those learning to ride, are sometimes impatient to move from their riding lessons on the 'flat' to their first lesson over jumps. But one is just a continuation of the other, and all training is important. It is the work done in the school, manège or paddock that eventually leads to success.

The fences used in show jumping, unlike the obstacles found when jumping cross-country, are built in such a way that they can be knocked down, without causing damage. No 'fixed' fences are permitted.

In either show jumping or jumping cross-country, the three parts of the jumping sequence are the same. They are the approach, the suspension and the landing. They may take years to. understand properly, and years longer to master. Jumping requires patience and good instruction. Skill will come in time, with patience. It will not be gained suddenly.

The act of jumping
The first requirement in jumping is to understand the 'act of jumping'. This act is best seen when horses or ponies are jumping 'free', without a rider. They make everything look so easy, always arriving at the right point in front of an obstacle, always appearing not to pause before jumping, and moving quite freely as they take off and land.

The horse or pony will, as the obstacle is approached, build up impulsion without any prompting. But the natural rhythmic action is, of course, upset when a rider is placed on the animal's back! Experienced riders know this: they have learnt to understand the action of the pony, and realize the part they have to play in allowing the pony to jump as freely as possible— as though the rider was not there. Those learning to jump may have problems in carrying out this role.

The importance of balance
Balance plays an important part in all aspects of riding. But so far as jumping is concerned, it is essential. Anything that upsets balance, especially as an obstacle is approached, can lead to a horse or pony refusing to jump, or avoiding having to jump by running away or running out. This form of disobedience, though penalized in show jumping and cross-country, can never be the fault of the horse or pony; for we know that horses will balance themselves perfectly without a rider.

In all practice sessions, the rider's aim should be to improve his or her own jumping skill and ability. It is unfortunate that there is no other way to learn to jump than by being taught on a horse or pony who probably knows what should be done, and would, in fact, do it if he were left alone to do it himself.

The rider's position when jumping

The rider's jumping position is critical. It must be taught in order to prevent development along wrong lines.

The body must remain still, the back and shoulders being moved slightly forward as the hands 'give' with the aid. The weight is taken on the knees and thighs. The stirrup irons must not be used as a means of support.

The leathers will be shorter, bringing the knees to a forward position. This assists the rider's own balance and enables a better grip to be made by the knees and thighs.

The rider must never look down in the act of jumping. The head must be kept looking straight ahead, for the slightest movement, whether of the head, body, legs, arms or hands, may easily upset the balance of the horse or pony.

The rider's legs remain close to the sides of the horse or pony, and the arms close to the rider's body. As the pace in-

Above: The hindlegs of this horse have just left the ground and the rider is in a very good position. A guide to determine the 'point of take-off' – shown here – is that it should be approximately the same distance as the height of the obstacle.

creases, the arms, shoulders and body follow the movement and adopt a more forward-looking position.

Trotting poles

In the first stage of the teaching of jumping, poles are laid in a line on the ground. By walking and trotting over the poles, the rider quickly learns to recognize the balance of the horse or pony, who, in turn, learns to accept the rider. The distance set between poles must be adjusted according to the stride pattern, but a guide would be to begin by having them spaced between 1.3 metres (4 ft 6 ins) and 1.5 metres (5 ft). The spacing will seem somewhat restricting after exercise and schooling in the wider spaces afforded by a paddock or manège.

As the horse or pony walks through the line of poles, the rider should 'give' as the animal's neck is stretched. The rider allows a free walk at the beginning of the exercise trying not to restrict the forward movement.

The rider begins by walking a line of, say, six poles. He turns on a left rein after the last pole, and walks back, keeping an even pace, to the point at which he started. Then he goes down the line again, but this time turns on a right rein, after the last pole. Spending at the most 20 minutes on the exercising and introducing as much variety as possible will be of great benefit.

When the horse or pony moves smoothly through the line of poles at all paces, the time has come to ask him to jump. It is a good idea before asking for an actual jump to raise the poles a little above the ground, perhaps by placing them on bricks. The horse or pony is taken through this line in the same way as when the poles were laid on the ground. Even at this low height a rider learning to jump will sense something of the act of jumping.

Using cavaletti

It is now time to add a cavaletto at the end of the line, spaced at the same distance as the poles. Later, its pace can be taken by a simple practice fence, preferably made with coloured poles.

A cavaletto is one of the most useful items of equipment to be found in a paddock or school. It is not difficult to construct one.

First, the cavaletto should be set at the lowest height (25 cm; 10 in) and the horse or pony should trot down the line of poles and then over the cavaletto. Patience is essential. The novice rider cannot expect a horse or pony to jump without some hesitation, especially if the novice rider is new to jumping and still somewhat nervous and apprehensive.

The next step is to put down a line of four or six cavaletti, and for the horse or pony to begin with the lowest height and progress to the higher one. In front of the cavaletti, one or two poles should be properly spaced.

Below: Poles laid on the ground at measured distances form the most useful grid for exercising both horse and rider. The distance between poles can be adjusted according to the stride. Use the poles without adding a cavalletto or low fence, and introduce this additional factor once the exercise on the flat is completed.

Making a cavaletto

Cavaletti are not difficult to make. Use lengths of timber 8 × 8 cm (3 × 3 in) square. Cut them into 1 metre (3 ft 3 in) lengths. You need four for each cavaletto. These are bolted across each other to form end-pieces. A further length of timber about 2.5 metres (8 feet) long is fixed across the endpieces. When properly constructed the height of the crossbar can be varied by turning over the cavaletto. At the highest it should be about 50 cm (20 in); at the lowest, 25 cm (10 in).

Above: A cavaletto is a simple practice fence. Here the versatility of these fences is clearly shown.

Below: A pony is seen jumping a low upright fence after having gone through a line of coloured poles.

Above: Once the horse or pony has shown he can cope with a single obstacle, the time will have come to introduce a simple double or combination. Here a one stride double is made up from two upright fences. The distance between each element will be that as shown (note that the photograph appears misleading – the distance between elements must never be set to 'trick' a horse or rider.)

Approach and take-off

The position of a horse or pony, as it arrives in front of an obstacle, should be such that it can take-off and jump without having to attempt to slow down or change pace. The 'point of take-off' varies according to the type of obstacle being faced. For example, some horses and ponies jump upright fences best when standing

Right: A well-balanced approach to an upright fence. The rider is obviously in a good position, and the horse would appear ready and willing to tackle the obstacle.

Left: At the point of take off the rider moves her body weight forward and allows the horse to have more use of his neck. At this time it is essential that the balance of the horse and rider is not upset.

back, others find it easier if they are nearer to the fence when about to jump.

Ponies, if left alone, will frequently get themselves out of trouble by adding an extra half-stride at the very last moment. But horses have to be positioned correctly at the point of take-off, any adjustment to the stride having to be made several strides before the fence is reached.

Ideally, the point of take-off should be such that a horse or pony will jump in a smooth arc, known as the *trajectory*. There is a risk when standing back that the hind legs of the pony will 'hook' a top pole and bring it down. Standing back is sometimes called 'taking off too early'. The opposite is to take off too late, or to get 'underneath' an obstacle. The effect

Left: After a short period of suspension, when the horse and rider are in the air and over the jump, the horse lands. Notice the rider's position: she will quietly come back into the saddle before 'collecting' her horse and moving on.

take the top element as the horse or pony is rising in the act of jumping.

Practice fences

There are four basic categories of fences and obstacles (other than water jumps): the upright or vertical fence; fences that have an ascending form; the hog's back or pyramid: and the parallel.

Practice fences used at home should be constructed to one or other of these designs. The aim should be to make obstacles inviting to jump and solid-looking. A groundline should be intro-duced if possible, perhaps by having a pole lying just in front of the upright. A horse uses the groundline to judge the height of a fence.

All jumps should be 'filled in,' avoiding anything open, and if possible there should be wings at either side of the fence.

When at practice over fences, the rider should always try to have someone else present. Apart from occasionally being able to assist, he or she can make any adjustments required to poles, spreads or cavaletti, and will be at hand should any accident happen.

Above: Standing back at the first part of a double will mean the horse having to 'put in' an almost impossible half-stride.

Above: Getting 'underneath', or taking off too near to the first element will, in a different way, mean a half stride is necessary to be able to take-off correctly for the second element.

Above: Taking off correctly will show how this two stride double can be jumped without asking the horse for any 'extra'.

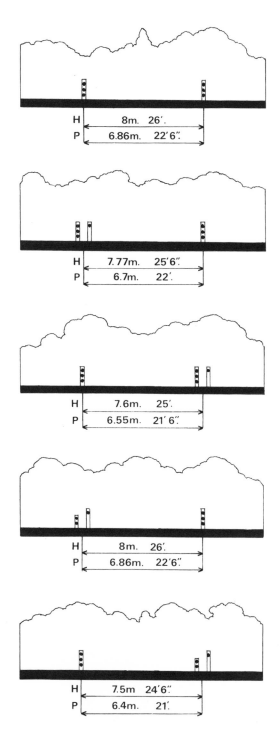

H	8m.	26'.
P	6.86m.	22'6".

H	7.77m.	25'6".
P	6.7m.	22'.

H	7.6m.	25'.
P	6.55m.	21'6".

H	8m.	26'.
P	6.86m.	22'6".

H	7.5m	24'6".
P	6.4m.	21'.

Above: The distances at which various types of combinations should be placed to be jumped by a horse (H) or by a pony (P).

Above: Two examples of the sort of spread fences that may be found in show jumping arenas.

Below: Studs like this can be fitted to the heels of shoes to give better grip while jumping. This is a simple job which can be done with an ordinary spanner.

7 : Competitive riding

In the showing rings today, there are classes for all breeds and sizes of horses and ponies. There are also classes specifically for stallions, mares, colts and foals. In all cases, the age of the horse or pony is stated: apart from foals or other young stock, the youngest age permitted to be shown is four years.

In spite of the high standards now generally set, there is a tremendous amount of fun to be had at the smaller, local shows. Showing a horse or pony is, like show jumping, a very competitive sport, and winning one day does not necessarily mean winning the next.

Showing classes

Showing classes fall into two categories: those for ridden horses ('under saddle') and those for led horses ('in hand'). The quality of entry very much depends on the show being attended: the pony kept at grass in the field at the end of the road can hardly be expected to stand up against the highly bred and versatile ponies shown in major rings throughout the world.

Every horse show produces a schedule setting out the classes to be held. The schedule gives the rules and conditions under which the classes are to be judged. The rules specify the heights of the animals allowed to compete in each class, the breed, the age and, sometimes whether or not a pony that has won more than a certain amount of money is eligible to compete. A pony's height—often called in question—can be established by securing a height certificate from the national body governing equestrian sport.

The judges will also look at manners,

Below: Show jumping is one phase in Horse Trials. At a three-day event, the show jumping competition comes after the dressage and cross-country phases.

Showing Classes

The classes found in the smaller, local shows include:

1 Breed classes: ponies registered with their Breed Society, up to a certain height and being ridden by riders of specified ages.

2 Mountain and Moorland classes: for ponies not registered with their Breed Society, and judged against each other.

3 Best condition and turn-out, a class usually divided into two: for grass-kept ponies, and for stable-kept ponies.

4 Leading rein: when the rider, who must not exceed a scheduled age, is led by a leading rein throughout the judging phase.

5 Children's Riding Pony, Child's First Pony and some of the Side-saddle classes: usually separate classes judged according to the stipulated height and age of the rider. Most schedules will insist that the ponies are mares or geldings and at least four years of age.

6 Working Hunter Pony: a popular competition judged according to the rules laid down by the British Show Pony Society (BSPS). All competitors must jump a number of natural-looking obstacles, and be prepared to give a display of their ability to ride and the pony's ability to answer and obey the aids given. The competition after the judging stage is judged on manners, freedom of action and conformation.

In the adult area, there are many classes, judged according to the rules of the various societies. An entrant may have to be a member of the relevant society, and the pony registered. These classes include those for Hunters, Hacks, Cobs, Riding Horse and Arabs.

not only of the pony but of the rider or handler. The turn-out is critical, and some hours of preparation, which usually has to be around dawn, can help to put one pony a shade higher than another.

To the uninitiated, the showing classes are complicated; they become easier to understand when you have attended one or two shows. This is not to say that you will necessarily agree with the judges' verdict: they may be taking into consideration points that you have not spotted. But visiting shows does give you a chance to gauge what the judges seem to be looking for.

What the judges see

Presentation is perhaps the most important thing in the show ring. Every aspect of the way the horse or pony is shown to the judges is taken into account and must be considered: the way the plaits have been prepared; the neatness and

Right: Showing competitions are always fun, especially those in which younger riders with well prepared and presented ponies take part.

cleanliness of the tack; the trimming and overall appearance.

The riders or handlers, too, are important in a show. It is no use a pony being perfectly turned-out if the rider is not.

Showing must be fun, even though some feel that the same few always seem to be 'in the ribbons'. 'There is always another day' is a comment heard frequently among the owners, a comment that should be shared by all the younger and less experienced riders who–whether they gain a prize or not–should feel rewarded just by having the fun of taking part.

Competitive jumping

Before entering a competition at a horse show, the rider or handler should have closely studied the schedule. This will indicate the various classes being staged, and will show whether or not they are planned for horses or ponies, for novice

or experienced riders. In the schedule will also be found the height of the fences for each jumping competition, another point to consider before making an entry.

Overfacing (asking a horse or pony to jump higher than he can) or underfacing (asking a horse or pony to jump fences far too low for his ability) can cause problems in the mind of an animal. It is best to jump within sensible limits, and to accept that only by perserverance and patience is one able to compete in the bigger classes.

On arrival at a showground, the rider must first see that all is well with the horse or pony. When the horse has been removed from the horse box or trailer, he must be checked to see that he has travelled well and that his shoes are firmly in position.

With the horse or pony tied up, the rider will go to the show secretary's tent to collect a riding number and to see that correct entries have been recorded. Then, before the start of any competition, he will have to report to the steward. In show jumping, this takes place in the collecting ring. In showing classes, the steward will usually be standing at the entrance to the ring. A collecting ring steward will register the rider's number, telling him when he will be expected to jump.

Perhaps ten minutes or so before a class starts, an announcement will be made inviting competitors to 'walk the course' To do so, they should be properly dressed. In the few minutes available to walk a course, they must study each of the fences in the order they will be jumped.

A rider should never be lazy at this time of a show, for it is the most important part of the day as far as the competitors are concerned. This is the one opportunity they will have to examine the fences and see what is being asked. They must work out the relative distances, study the combination obstacles, measure strides between fences, and plan where they will turn at corners. They must also study the jump-off course, for they will not be

allowed to walk this shortened and raised course if they have a clear first round.

Horse trials

As the rider gains experience, there are other equestrian activities to be enjoyed, including horse trials (until recently called *eventing*). The very experienced riders have *three-day horse trials*, which have one day given over to a dressage phase, the second to cross-country and the third to show jumping.

One-day trials usually set the dressage and show jumping phases in the morning, with the cross-country course jumped during the afternoon.

All levels of experience are catered for in horse trials, from the beginner to the most advanced. And, for those who would rather not face a cross-country course, there are combined training competitions. These comprise a dressage test followed by one round of show jumping.

On the other hand, there are many riders who love jumping cross-country. For these, there are hunter trials, at which there is no dressage or show jumping.

Above: An international competitor taking part in the dressage phase at a three-day Event.

The dressage phase

Dressage is training a horse to perform movements requiring obedience, skill and exactitude.

When learning to ride many younger people feel they will never be able to compete in dressage competitions. The whole business of dressage appears extremely complicated and does not carry the excitement of jumping. But, if dressage is thought of as a series of grouped schooling tests, it will make it easier to understand why this discipline of equestrian sport is becoming increasingly popular.

The cross-country phase

Jumping a cross-country course demands a somewhat different technique from that used in show jumping. As each obstacle is 'fixed'–that is, it will not fall down when hit–a far more determined approach must be adopted. Depending on the competition, there may be as many as 20 obstacles to be jumped. Each obstacle is designed and built to be as natural as possible. There are gates, ditches, fallen trees, rustic fences, water hazards, hedges and walls—the types of obstacles found when hunting or truly riding across country.

The rules are not involved. But this part of one-day or three-day trials demands courage, determination and skill.

Competitors will walk the course before the competition to discover what is being asked of them and their mounts. The speed of the competition will be known. This will be much faster than that common in show jumping arenas. Penalties are awarded against horses or ponies (or riders) who fall, refuse or run out, or who commit other faults listed in the schedule.

A rider who is eliminated is asked to leave the course and return to the horse box lines by another route. A horse who is going slowly or has had one or two refusals must give way to any horse or pony that is following.

Below: Probably the toughest of all aspects of riding is to compete at top level in the cross-country phase of a Horse Trials. Here, a competitor clears one of the 'fixed' fences in a novice competition.

Index